CONVERSATIONS
WITH SCRIPTURE:
THE GOSPEL
OF MARK

CONVERSATIONS
WITH SCRIPTURE:

THE GOSPEL OF MARK

MARCUS BORG

Morehouse Publishing

An imprint of Church Publishing Incorporated

HARRISBURG—NEW YORK

Morehouse Publishing, 4775 Linglestown Road, Harrisburg, PA 17112

Morehouse Publishing, 445 Fifth Avenue, New York, NY 10016

Morehouse Publishing is an imprint of Church Publishing Incorporated.

Cover art: Veneziano, Lorenzo (fl.1356–1379), *Saint Mark*, Accademia, Venice, Italy; courtesy of Cameraphoto Arte, Venice/Art Resource, NY

Cover design by Jennifer Glosser

Library of Congress Cataloging-in-Publication Data

Borg, Marcus J.
    Conversations with Scripture : the Gospel of Mark / Marcus Borg.
        p.   cm. — (Anglican Association of Biblical Scholars study series)
    Includes bibliographical references.
    ISBN 978-0-8192-2339-5 (pbk.)
    1. Bible. N.T. Mark—Criticism, interpretation, etc. I. Title.
BS2585.52.B67   2009
226.3'06—dc22
                                                            2009015616

Printed in the United States of America

10 11 12 13 14   10 9 8 7 6 5 4 3

*To Frank and Mimsy Jones
and the community at Calvary Episcopal Church
in Memphis, Tennessee.*

*With thanksgiving for their generous
hospitality over the years.*

A Prayer from Alcuin (around 800 AD)

Give us, O Lord, we pray:
Firm faith,
Unwavering hope,
A passion for justice.

Pour into our hearts:
The spirit of wisdom and understanding,
The spirit of counsel and spiritual strength,
The spirit of knowledge and true compassion,
And the spirit of wonder in all your works.

Light eternal, shine in our hearts;
Power eternal, deliver us from evil;
Wisdom eternal, scatter the darkness of our ignorance;
Might eternal, have mercy on us.

Grant that we may ever seek your face,
With all our heart and soul and strength;
And in your infinite mercy,
Bring us at last to the fullness of your presence
Where we shall behold your glory
And live your promised joys.

THROUGH JESUS CHRIST OUR LORD, AMEN

A prayer from Augustine (around 400 AD)

O God, from whom to be turned is to fall,
To whom to be turned is to rise,
And in whom to stand is to abide forever:
Grant us in all our duties thy help.
In all our perplexities thy guidance.
In all our dangers thy protection,
And in all our sorrow thy peace.

THROUGH JESUS CHRIST OUR LORD, AMEN

CONTENTS

INTRODUCTION
TO THE SERIES

To talk about a distinctively Anglican approach to Scripture is a daunting task. Within any one part of the larger church that we call the Anglican Communion there is, on historical grounds alone, an enormous variety. But as the global character of the church becomes apparent in ever-newer ways, the task of accounting for that variety, while naming the characteristics of a distinctive approach, becomes increasingly difficult.

In addition, the examination of Scripture is not confined to formal studies of the kind addressed in this series of parish studies written by formally trained biblical scholars. Systematic theologian David Ford, who participated in the 1998 Lambeth Conference, rightly noted that although "most of us have studied the Bible over many years" and "are aware of various academic approaches to it," we have "also lived in it" and "inhabited it, through worship, preaching, teaching, and meditation." As such, Ford observes, "The Bible in the Church is like a city we have lived in for a long time." We may not be able to account for the history of every building or the architecture on every street, but we know our way around and it is a source of life to each of us.[1]

That said, we have not done as much as we should in acquainting the inhabitants of that famed city with the architecture that lies within. So, as risky as it may seem, it is important to describe the sights and sounds of the city we call the Bible that matter most to its Anglican residents.

The first of those descriptors that leaps to mind is familiar, basic, and forever debated: *authoritative.* Years ago I was asked by a colleague who belonged to the Evangelical Free Church why someone with as much obvious interest in the Bible would be an Episcopal priest. I responded, "Because we read the whole of Scripture and not just the parts of it that suit us." Scripture has been and continues to play a singular role in the life of the Anglican Communion, but it has rarely been used in the sharply prescriptive fashion that has characterized some traditions.

Some have characterized this approach as an attempt to navigate a *via media* between overbearing control and an absence of accountability. But I think it is far more helpful to describe the tensions not as a matter of steering a course between two different and competing priorities, but as the complex dance necessary to live under a very different, but typically Anglican notion of authority itself. Authority shares the same root as the word "to author" and as such refers first and foremost, not to the *power* to *control* with all that both of those words suggest, but to the capacity to *author creativity,* with all that both of those words suggest.[2] As such, the function of Scripture is to carve out a creative space in which the work of the Holy Spirit can yield the very kind of fruit associated with its work in the church. The difficulty, of course, is that for that space to be creative, it is also necessary for it to have boundaries, much like the boundaries we establish for other kinds of genuinely creative freedom: the practice of scales for concert pianists, the discipline of work at the barre that frees the ballerina, or the guidance that parents provide for their children. Defined in this way, it is possible to see the boundaries around that creative space as barriers to be eliminated, or as walls that provide protection, but they are neither.

And so the struggle continues with the authority of Scripture. From time to time in the Anglican Communion, it has been and will be treated as a wall that protects us from the complexity of navigating without error the world in which we live. At other times, it will be treated as the ancient remains of a city to be cleared away in favor of a brave new world. But both approaches are rooted, not in the limitations of Scripture, but in our failure to welcome the creative space we have been given.

For that reason, at their best, Anglican approaches to Scripture are also *illuminative.* William Sloane Coffin once observed that the problem with Americans and the Bible is that we read it like a drunk uses a lamppost. We lean on it, we don't use it for illumination.[3] Leaning on Scripture and having the lamppost taken out completely are simply two very closely related ways of failing to acknowledge the creative space provided by Scripture. But once the creative space is recognized for what it is, then the importance of reading Scripture for illumination becomes apparent. Application of the insight Scripture provides into who we are and what we might become is not something that can be prescribed or mapped out in detail. It is only a conversation with Scripture, marked by humility, that can begin to spell out the particulars. Reading Scripture is, then, in the Anglican tradition a delicate and demanding task, that involves both the careful listening for the voice of God and courageous conversation with the world around us.

It is, for that reason, an approach that is also marked by *critical engagement* with the text itself. It is no accident that from 1860 to 1900 the three best-known names in the world of biblical scholarship were Anglican priests, the first two of whom were bishops: B. F. Westcott, J. B. Lightfoot, and F. J. A. Hort. Together the three made contributions to both the church and the critical study of the biblical text that became a defining characteristic of Anglican life.

Of the three, Westcott's contribution, perhaps, best captures the balance. Not only did his work contribute to a critical text of the Greek New Testament that would eventually serve as the basis for the English Revised Version, but as Bishop of Durham he also convened a conference of Christians to discuss the arms race in Europe, founded the Christian Social Union, and mediated the Durham coal strike of 1892.

The English roots of the tradition are not the only, or even the defining, characteristic of Anglican approaches to Scripture. The church, no less than the rest of the world, has been forever changed by the process of globalization, which has yielded a rich *diversity* that complements the traditions once identified with the church.

Scripture in Uganda, for example, has been read with an emphasis on private, allegorical, and revivalist applications. The result has been a tradition in large parts of East Africa that stresses the reading of Scripture on one's own: the direct application made to the contemporary situation without reference to the setting of the original text; and the combination of personal testimony with the power of public exhortation.

At the same time, however, globalization has brought that tradition into conversation with people from other parts of the Anglican Communion, as the church in Uganda has sought to bring the biblical text to bear on its efforts to address the issues of justice, poverty, war, disease, food shortage, and education. In such a dynamic environment, the only thing that one can say with certainty is that neither the Anglican Communion, nor the churches of East Africa, will ever be the same again.

Authoritative, illuminative, critical, and varied—these are not the labels that one uses to carve out an approach to Scripture that can be predicted with any kind of certainty. Indeed, if the word *dynamic* is added to the list, perhaps all that one can predict is still more change! But such is the nature of life in any city, including one shaped by the Bible. We influence the shape of its life, but we are also shaped and nurtured by it. And if that city is of God's making, then to force our own design on the streets and buildings around us is to disregard the design that the chief architect has in mind.

—Frederick W. Schmidt
Series Editor

AUTOBIOGRAPHICAL NOTE

This book is the product of the two longest-lasting commitments of my life. I am in my seventh decade as a Christian and in my fifth decade as a student and teacher of religion. I was a Christian before I could walk or talk. I began the serious study of religion in my twenties and for about forty years, I have taught in colleges, universities, seminaries, and churches.

Much of my life has been about the relationship between these two commitments: the role of reason and the intellect in the life of Christian faith—that is, the relationship between faith and reason. Christians have seen this relationship in very different ways. Some see faith and reason as rivals, even enemies; some see them as partners.

The Lutheran tradition in which I grew up was ambivalent about the relationship. It was suspicious of reason and yet also valued it. In his colorful language, Martin Luther spoke of reason as "a whore"—it could be prostituted to serve any cause. He was right. On the other hand, in his courageous and famous statement when he stood before an imperial and ecclesiastical court with the power to condemn him to death, Luther said, "Here I stand. I can do no other. Unless I am convinced by Scripture *and evident reason*, I cannot and will not recant." To say the obvious, reason mattered greatly. He was right again.

My teenage years were marked by experiencing faith and reason as rivals. Much of what I was learning about the world, in school and elsewhere, conflicted with the understanding of Christianity that I had acquired in childhood. So, did faith mean that I should continue believing those understandings, even though some of them no longer made persuasive sense? I suspect that most Christians who grew up in the twentieth century have experienced something like this. I remember praying frequently, "I believe—help thou my unbelief." Reason, I feared, was leading me away from faith.

The rest of my life has persuaded me that faith and reason need not be rivals. Rather, they can be partners, indeed, need to be partners. Faith without reason can become fantasy and, at its extreme, fanaticism. Reason without faith can become arid and amoral. This book, I trust, illustrates the fruit that reason and faith as partners can produce.

Though I grew up Lutheran, I am now an Episcopalian. In my twenties, several years of graduate study in England involved me more and more in Anglican worship—there aren't many Lutherans in England. I especially loved evensong in the ancient college chapels of Oxford.

Back in the States, for a number of reasons, I did not have much involvement in a church during most of my thirties. Then, around forty, I began to attend Episcopal worship services. I was attracted by the liturgy, the Book of Common Prayer, and the rich, broad theology of the Anglican tradition. Soon I was confirmed as an Episcopalian. The Episcopal Church has provided a nourishing spiritual home ever since. I am grateful.

From my Christian and intellectual journey has come my vocational passion: introducing Christians and seekers to a way of seeing Christianity—including the Bible, the gospels, and Jesus—that makes persuasive and compelling sense. In particular, my passion is adult theological re-education. Such re-education needs to happen at the congregational level. It is a crucial task.

The reason: a way of seeing Christianity that was very common a generation or two ago and that many of us grew up with has ceased to be persuasive to millions. Many are still within churches and looking for a persuasive alternative. Many have left. Some of them might be interested in coming back, if only....

So we are fortunate to live in a time when another way of seeing Christianity is emerging. Its results are encouraging. Millions of Christians who experienced difficulties carrying their childhood beliefs about the Bible and the gospels into their adult lives have found this way of seeing to be enormously helpful, illuminating, and rich.

In thousands of congregations, mostly in mainline Protestant denominations, this emerging way has been a means of revitalizing and deepening Christian understanding and commitment. It is a way that integrates faith and reason, head and heart, intellect, experience, and yearning. For me, it has made all the difference. This book is a small contribution to this process of adult theological re-education.

Around the year 70, in the first century—some four decades after the historical life of Jesus—an early Christian put the story of Jesus into writing for the first time. During those forty-or-so years, in Christian communities in the Jewish homeland and beyond, accounts about Jesus existed only in oral form and were told as individual stories.

Now, for the first time, those stories were put into writing as a sequential narrative with a beginning, a middle, and an end. Though the author did not call his manuscript a "gospel," and did not write his name on the title page, what he wrote became known as "The Gospel of Mark."

"Gospel" translates a Greek word that meant "good news." The word did not yet mean a document or a literary genre when Mark wrote. But soon, and because of Mark, that is the meaning it took on, as when we speak of the four gospels of Mark, Matthew, Luke, and John. But initially, it meant an oral or written proclamation of "good news" about something that had happened. Because of Mark, it began to mean a type of document, a particular literary form or genre, even as it also retained the meaning of a proclamation.

The Importance of Mark

Mark is important in part because of its status as the earliest gospel. In the New Testament, only the genuine letters of Paul, written in the fifties, are earlier. But they are letters, not gospels, addressing questions and conflicts within early Christian communities. Paul's letters do not tell the story of Jesus; that was not their purpose. Paul had already told these communities about the gospel—the good news—

of Jesus when he was with them in person. That makes Mark the first to tell the story of Jesus *in writing*.

Mark is important for a second reason: it is the primary source for two other gospels, Matthew and Luke. When the authors of these subsequent gospels wrote a decade or two later, they used Mark as one of their sources. About ninety percent of Mark is also in Matthew and about two-thirds of Mark is in Luke.

Synoptic gospels: the gospels of Mark, Luke, and Matthew, so called because they are quite similar

Because these three gospels are quite similar, they are known as the *synoptic gospels*. Both Matthew and Luke supplemented Mark's narrative with other material, primarily with a collection of the teachings of Jesus composed of short sayings and parables. Most scholars think this collection existed in written form as a document that is called "Q." Thus, as the fountainhead of the synoptics, Mark provides the narrative form of the story of Jesus in three of the four New Testament gospels. (The gospel of John, not one of the synoptics, tells the story of Jesus quite differently.)

But despite Mark's importance as the earliest gospel, it has been relatively neglected in the life of the church for much of Christian history. Until a few decades ago, Mark did not often appear in the readings assigned for Sunday mornings. Instead, gospel texts most often came from Matthew and John and, less often, from Luke. Only recently has Mark received its own year in the three-year cycle of Sunday gospel readings. Because of this relative neglect, the distinctive features of Mark's gospel have not until recently been part of common Christian understandings of Jesus and the gospels.

Mark's Distinctiveness

Mark has a number of distinctive features that make its study not only important but surprising. Given that Mark is the first to put the story of Jesus into written form, he surprises us by what he does *not* include:

- Mark does not begin with stories of the birth of Jesus, as Matthew and Luke do. Instead, he begins with Jesus as an adult going to John the Baptizer in the wilderness.
- Mark does not contain some of the most familiar teachings of Jesus: the Sermon on the Mount, the Lord's Prayer, and

well-known parables like the Good Samaritan and the Prodigal Son.

- Mark does not portray Jesus as proclaiming his identity as Son of God and Messiah. Of course, Mark affirms that Jesus is both, but not as part of the message of Jesus himself. The few such affirmations in Mark occur "in private"—they were not part of Jesus' public teaching.
- Mark does not have any stories of the risen Jesus appearing to his followers. Appearance stories are found only in the other gospels. Instead, Mark ends with the story of the empty tomb.

I mention these features not for the sake of casting doubts on Mark, but to emphasize that studying Mark involves seeing the distinctiveness of this gospel.

The Perspective of This Book

How we see matters. How we see is a function of our perspective, our vantage point. The vantage point of this book integrates the two perspectives that have shaped the way I see the Bible and the gospels: I am a Christian and a mainstream biblical scholar.

A CHRISTIAN PERSPECTIVE

For me as a Christian, Jesus is *the decisive revelation of God.* This is Christianity's most central claim and it goes back to its beginnings. In language from the New Testament, Jesus is "the image of the invisible God" (Col 1:15), "the Word of God" incarnate (John 1:1–14), "the Light of the World" (John 9:5), God's revelation to Jews and Gentiles alike (Luke 2:32–33). Jesus *reveals, discloses, embodies* what can be seen of God in a human life.

This claim distinguishes Christianity from other religions. To use our two nearest relatives to illustrate this point, Jews find the decisive revelation of God in a book—in the Jewish Bible, especially the Torah (the first five books of the Bible, also known as the books of Moses, the Law, and the Pentateuch) and commentaries on it (the Mishnah and Talmud). So also Muslims find the decisive revelation of God in a book, the Quran. But Christians find the decisive revelation of God not in a book, but in a person: Jesus.

This distinction is not about superiority, but about difference. It has an immediate implication. Given Jesus' centrality for Christians, it matters immensely how we see Jesus and the gospels that tell his story. If Jesus shows us what can be seen of God in a human life—well, what was he like?

A MAINSTREAM SCHOLARLY PERSPECTIVE

The second perspective that shapes the vantage point of this book is mainstream biblical scholarship. It is a way of seeing the Bible and the gospels that began in the Enlightenment of the seventeenth and eighteenth centuries and has continued to develop to this day.

This perspective is shared by scholars within "the mainstream academy"—those whose approach to the study of religion and the Bible is taught in public and private universities and colleges where faculty are not required to adhere to specific Christian doctrines. This approach does not begin with a commitment to Christian beliefs, whether those beliefs are based on twenty-first-century American Christianity, or the sixteenth-century Reformation, or the fourth-century Nicene Creed. This perspective is shared by scholars whatever their religious orientation, and by those with no particular religious orientation at all.

> **The mainstream academy:** those whose approach to the study of religion and the Bible does not require them to adhere to any specific Christian doctrine

Some of you have encountered this kind of scholarship in university or college courses in religious studies. It is also the kind of biblical scholarship taught in most mainline Protestant and Catholic seminaries—at some institutions for more than a century; at others for only a generation or two. It is central to the theological foundation of what is increasingly called in our time "emerging" or "progressive" Christianity.

> **Emerging or progressive Christianity:** combines what has sometimes been called "liberal" Christianity with a strong spiritual emphasis, commitment, and practice

This way of seeing the Bible and the gospels is quite different from what many of us who grew up in the church learned early in life. Many of us formed the impression, whether explicitly taught or only implied, that the Bible is a divine product. Pronouncements that the Bible is "the Word of God" and "inspired by God" were understood to mean that the Bible comes from God in a way that no other book does. That is why the Bible matters: it has the authority of God and thus a divine guarantee to be true.

Within this framework, the Bible's truth is most often understood to include both historical factuality and moral absolutes. If the Bible says something happened, it happened; if the Bible says something is wrong, it's wrong. Many of us also got the impression that the Bible should be interpreted literally, unless there are obvious reasons to do otherwise.

Some Christians insist that this is the only Christian way of seeing the Bible—a test of Christian orthodoxy. Some have been able to retain this way of seeing the Bible into adulthood. Some have not, but think they should. And some have found another way of seeing the Bible shaped by mainstream biblical scholarship. Its foundations include:

- The Bible is a human product, not a divine product. It is the product of two ancient communities. The Jewish Bible—what Christians call the Old Testament—is the product of ancient Israel. The New Testament is the product of the early Christian movement. To see the Bible as the work of human beings does not deny the reality of God, or the reality that the Bible was divinely inspired. But the Bible is not a divine product. Rather, it's a collection of writings by our spiritual ancestors, the biblical ancestors of the Christian tradition. It tells us how they experienced the sacred, saw the world, told their stories, and understood what life with God involved.
- The Bible is not to be interpreted literally, factually, and absolutely. Its language is often metaphorical, and its primary concern is not factual reporting. Its laws and ethical teaching are not absolutes relevant to all times and places, but are the products of those ancient communities and address their time and place. This does not mean that its laws and ethics are irrelevant to our time. But they cannot simply be directly transferred to the twenty-first century.
- Seeing the Bible this way does not deny its status as Christian sacred Scripture. Instead, this viewpoint holds that Scripture

is sacred not because of its origin, but because our spiritual ancestors canonized it—that is, declared it to be sacred. As sacred Scripture, the Bible is, along with Jesus, the foundation of Christian understanding and identity. It is also a way that the Spirit of God continues to speak to us today. Thus the Bible is *sacred scripture in its status and function, but not in origin*— not because it comes from God as no other book does.

From personal experience and the testimony of many, I am convinced that this way of seeing the Bible (including Mark and the other gospels) offers a way of re-claiming its power and meaning. It emphasizes understanding rather than belief, even as it also acknowledges the limits of understanding. There is always more.

Mark within the Perspective of Mainstream Scholarship

In a sentence, Mark is seen by mainstream scholars as the product of developing early Christian traditions about Jesus and it combines memory, interpretation, and metaphor. We now unpack this sentence.

A DEVELOPING TRADITION

Seeing Mark (and the other gospels) as the product of a developing tradition means something very simple. As mentioned earlier, Mark is the earliest gospel, written around forty years after the historical life of Jesus. During those four decades, the traditions about Jesus developed. It is clear from the gospels themselves that the followers of Jesus understood him more fully after Easter than they did before Easter. Their conviction that God had raised Jesus and that he continued to be known affected their understanding of his significance decisively. They also adapted and applied the traditions about Jesus.

Here are three examples of the way the Christian tradition developed:

- *Peter's declaration of Jesus' identity in Mark 8:27–30,* which we will look at in greater detail in Chapter 5. In this story, Jesus asks the disciples, "Who do you say that I am?" Peter answers, "You are the Messiah" (or "the Christ," which means the same thing).

As Matthew takes this story over from Mark a few years later, he adds to it in two ways. To Peter's affirmation that Jesus is the Messiah, Matthew 16:16 adds "the Son of the Living God." In the next two verses, 16:17–19, Matthew adds that Jesus responds to Peter:

Blessed are you, Simon son of Jonah! [Peter's name, before it became Peter]. For flesh and blood has not revealed this to you, but my Father in heaven. And I tell you, you are Peter [the name means "rock"], and on this rock I will build my church, and the gates of Hades shall not prevail against it. I will give you the keys of the kingdom of heaven, and whatever you bind on earth will be bound in heaven, and whatever you loose on earth will be loosed in heaven.

■ *Jesus' teaching about divorce and re-marriage.* Mark 10:11–12 forbids re-marriage after divorce: "Whoever divorces his wife and marries another commits adultery against her; and if she divorces her husband and marries another, she commits adultery." Matthew 19:9 changes Mark's absolute statement by adding an exception clause: "Whoever divorces his wife, *except for unchastity*, and marries another commits adultery."

■ *Jesus' entry into Jerusalem.* In Mark 11:1–10, Jesus rides into the city on a colt. As Matthew incorporates this story into his gospel in 21:1–11, he adds another, so that Jesus rides into Jerusalem on *two* animals, a donkey and a colt (21:2, 3, 7). Matthew adds the second animal to make the story conform to his reading of a passage from Zechariah 9:9 in the Jewish Bible, which he quotes in 21:5.

There are multiple examples of such development as Matthew and Luke use Mark to write their own stories of Jesus. It is easiest to see this by using a book of "gospel parallels," in which Matthew, Mark, and Luke are printed in parallel columns. The point: if development of the story of Jesus happened in the relatively short time between the writing of Mark and the writing of Matthew and Luke, then it is reasonable to assume that the story also developed before Mark was written.

As the product of a developing tradition, Mark and the other gospels contain the *testimony* of early Christians to the meaning and significance that Jesus had come to have in their lives in the decades since his historical life. And Mark and the other gospels also *adapt* and *apply* the traditions about Jesus to their communities in their time and place.

MEMORY AND INTERPRETATION

It's clear that Mark and the other gospels combine earlier and later layers of material about Jesus. As the product of developing traditions, they contain pre-Easter memories of Jesus and post-Easter interpretation of what his life meant. "Pre-Easter memory" means that some of what is in the gospels goes back to things Jesus said and did. "Post-Easter interpretation" means that some of what is in the gospels is the way early Christian traditions testified to—and applied—what they understood about Jesus. Both matter—we do not need to choose between them. But it's important and illuminating to see the difference.

> **Pre-Easter memory: parts of the gospels based on what Jesus actually said and did**

MEMORY AND METAPHOR

Mark also combines memory and metaphor, as do the other gospels—and biblical narratives generally. In its broad sense, the metaphorical meaning of language is its *more than literal, more than factual,* meaning.

I emphasize "more than" because of a common assumption in modern Western culture that metaphorical language is "less than" factual language. Many of us have heard people say when they hear that a biblical story might be metaphorical, "You mean it's *only* metaphorical, *only* symbolic?" The question reflects the way our culture equated truth with factuality.

But metaphorical language is not inferior to factual language. *Rather, metaphor is about meaning.* Metaphor is "the surplus of meaning" that language can carry, a phrase I owe to Paul Ricoeur, a twentieth-century scholar of religion. Metaphor and metaphorical narratives can be profoundly true—meaning-filled and meaningful, truthful and truth-filled. For example, the

> **Post-Easter interpretation: parts of the gospels based on early Christian tradition after Jesus' crucifixion**

parables of Jesus are all metaphorical narratives; their purpose is not to report an event that actually happened. But nobody dismisses them because they're not as factual as newspaper articles. Everybody recognizes that the parables are about meaning, and the same is true with metaphorical narratives in general.

Some metaphorical narratives combine memory and metaphor. That is, they reflect an event that really happened, but the reason the stories were remembered and told is because they were seen to have a more-than-historical meaning.

Metaphor: "the surplus of meaning" that language can carry

For example, consider the story of Israel's exodus from Egypt. Whatever historical memory lies behind that story, it was told not simply or primarily to report "what happened." Rather, its more-than-factual, more-than-literal meanings mattered most to ancient Israel, as they do for us. The story of Israel's flight from Egypt is a story of bondage to Pharaoh, liberation by God, journey through the wilderness, and arrival in "the promised land."

The story was—and continues to be—a metaphorical narrative of the human condition and the path of deliverance. It portrays the human condition with an image of bondage: we are not free, the story tells us, but enslaved by the Pharaohs who rule our lives. God's will is that we be liberated into a life under God rather than under the lords of this world. Together, bondage and liberation are powerful biblical metaphors for the human predicament—and its solution.

We turn to a second example of a biblical story that combines memory and metaphor. The Jewish experience of exile in Babylon happened in the 500s BCE. After half a century in exile, some Jews returned to their homeland. That is memory. But the language of exile and return is about more than memory. Like bondage, exile is a central biblical image for a larger experience—the sense of separation and estrangement that often marks our lives. When our problem is exile, this Bible story tells us, the solution is a journey of return.

Our third example of memory and metaphor comes from Mark: the story of Jesus' final journey to Jerusalem (8:22–10:52). Jesus really made that journey. But Mark overlays the story with a metaphorical meaning: our *own* journey of discipleship means following Jesus—on the way that leads to Jerusalem, death, and resurrection.

There is a second kind of metaphorical narrative in the Bible—those stories that are purely metaphorical, without elements of memory. A classic example is the Genesis story of Adam and Eve. Mainstream scholars do not think there ever was an Adam or Eve, a Garden of Eden, a tree of the knowledge of good and evil, or a talking serpent. And yet as a metaphorical narrative, the story of Adam and Eve is filled with meanings and truths. To echo Thomas Mann, it is a story about the way things never were, but always are. Like most metaphorical narratives, it has more than one meaning. Among its meanings: we begin our lives "in God," in paradise, but we live our lives "east of Eden," that is, outside of the felt presence of God, and we yearn to return.

The meaning and truth of metaphorical narratives are not dependent on their literal or historical factuality. They need not be based on the memory of something that happened.

To provide an illustration from Mark: the gospel has two stories of Jesus stilling a storm on the Sea of Galilee, and in one he also walks on the water (4:35–41, 6:45–52). For more than one reason, mainstream scholars do not think these stories are based on the memory of something that happened. They are purely metaphorical narratives. I will treat them in detail in Chapters 3 and 4, but for now I emphasize that a metaphorical approach does not focus on the factual question of whether Jesus really did still a storm and walk on water. Instead, it focuses on the more-than-factual meanings of these stories—on their meanings as metaphor.

Interpreting Mark: A Historical-Metaphorical Approach

How we interpret a biblical text matters greatly. To say anything at all about a text is to interpret it. This is true for everybody, including those who read biblical texts literally, factually, and absolutely. The Bible does not come with footnotes that tell us to interpret a text this way. Rather, doing so involves an interpretive decision, whether consciously or unconsciously made, to interpret the Bible literally, factually, and absolutely.

From mainstream scholarship's way of seeing Mark (and the Bible as a whole) flows a different way of interpreting the traditions that Mark put together in his gospel. In shorthand, this way of interpreting Mark involves a "historical-metaphorical approach."

In the nineteenth century, this was commonly called "the higher criticism" and in the twentieth century "the historical-critical method." The words "criticism" and "critical" distinguished this approach from pre-critical or non-critical ways of seeing the Bible. But calling it a "historical-metaphorical" approach better expresses the fullness and richness of this way of seeing the Bible.

> **Historical-critical:** an interpretive approach based on examining biblical stories within their ancient context

A *historical* approach means, very simply, setting biblical texts in their ancient historical contexts. To avoid a possible misunderstanding, let's be clear about what we don't mean by "historical." Sometimes, the word "historical" is used to refer to an event that happened, as when we ask if a story about our grandparents is true. "Is that historical?" we might ask our amateur family historian. "Did it *really* happen that way?" But that's not what we mean by a historical approach to the Bible and to the gospel of Mark. A historical approach is not intrinsically concerned with the question of factuality. Though it can address that question, it is seldom crucially important.

> **Historical-metaphorical:** an interpretive approach that combines a historical-critical approach with an emphasis on the more-than-factual meaning

Rather, the historical approach to the Bible means setting a text—whether a narrative, a hymn or prayer, poetry or parable, legal or ethical teaching—in the historical context of the life of the ancient community in which it originated. Doing so has great illuminating power.

Importantly, *historical context* is not simply "background" or "setting." It's *interactive*—time and place are not simply the background and setting in which we live, but they shape what we say and do.

For example, the American Civil War was not simply the "background" or the "setting" of Abraham Lincoln's presidential addresses; it was their *interactive* context. He would not have said what he said, or said it in the way that he did, apart from the interactive context of the Civil War. So also, a century later, American racism and the civil rights movement were not simply the "background" or "setting" of

Martin Luther King's memorable speeches and sermons—it was their *interactive context*. It shaped him and what he said.

We turn to how this affects our reading of Mark. A historical approach sets Mark's story of Jesus in the historical context in which this gospel was written around the year 70 C.E. What was going on in Mark's community and within the larger world of Judaism and the even larger world of the Roman Empire? What *did* the stories and teachings in Mark mean within those contexts?

This emphasis on the ancient meanings of biblical and gospel texts does not mean confining or reducing them to those ancient meanings. But it does mean that thinking about their meanings for us in our contemporary context begins with thinking about their ancient meanings. What does what *they meant then* suggest about *their meanings for our now*?

We've already looked at the foundations of a *metaphorical approach*. Using this approach helps us focus on the more-than-literal meaning of biblical and gospel narratives, developing a sensitivity to the meanings of a story. And the metaphorical approach is enhanced by the historical approach. That is, given what we know about the historical context, what more-than-factual, more-than-literal meanings do we see in this story?

Within this framework, we now turn to Mark. We focus on what we can know or surmise with reasonable probability about the authorship and interactive context of the earliest gospel.

Authorship, Community, and Historical Context

Authorship of the gospels means something very different from what authorship means today. In the modern world, authors commonly write books that are fresh and creative for an audience they do not know. Why else would people read them?

Not so for the authors of the gospels. They were written by "authors" who knew the people they were writing for—they were Christians living within Christian communities who put into writing the traditions and convictions of their communities. The author of Mark was not an individual innovator who hoped to find an audience for his book. Rather, Mark tells us how he *and* his community saw things—how they understood and told the story of Jesus.

THE AUTHOR OF MARK

So what do we know or what can we reasonably surmise about the author? None of the gospels originally mentioned its author. Whoever wrote Mark did not begin by writing "The Gospel According to Mark" at the top of the first page. Instead, the names of the gospels were added in the second century when early Christian communities began to need to differentiate the gospels from each other. Some (perhaps many) of these communities would have known of only one or two gospels until at least the end of the first century and probably later.

Yet it is likely that the gospel was written by a person named Mark. *Markos* (in Greek), or *Marcus* (in Latin), was a fairly common name in the first-century Mediterranean world, not only among Greeks and Romans but also among Jews. But none of the disciples or other prominent early Christians was named Mark. Thus there is no obvious reason why Christians in the second century would name this gospel "Mark" unless somebody named Mark had written it.

Until about fifty years ago, it was common to identify this Mark as a companion and interpreter of Peter, who was executed in Rome around the year 64. Shortly thereafter, according to Eusebius, a fourth-century Christian historian, Mark wrote his gospel in Rome and based it on Peter's teaching. Eusebius cites a tradition going back to a second-century bishop and martyr named Papias.

But in the past half century, scholars have become skeptical of this tradition. After all, it's third-hand information: Eusebius in the fourth century reported what Papias said in the second century about Mark in the first century. We also know that Papias was incorrect about other things he is reported to have said about the gospels. Thus most scholars now see the evidence for identifying the author with a companion of Peter and the location of its composition as Rome as problematic.

Instead, contemporary mainstream scholars seek to deduce what we can know about the gospel's author, audience, location, and time from internal evidence within the gospel itself. Internal evidence is now the basis for making an educated judgment—that is, a historical judgment with some degree of probability.

MARK'S AUDIENCE

Internal evidence suggests that the community (or communities) in which and for whom Mark wrote included both Christian Jews and Christian Gentiles (that is, non-Jews). That's because in this gospel, Jewish practices are sometimes briefly explained, which would not have been necessary if all or most of the community were Christian Jews. But neither was the community primarily made up of Christian Gentiles—there are many things in Mark that make no sense without an acquaintance with Judaism. Moreover, until well into the third century, the majority of Christians were of Jewish origin. In the first century, this was even more so.

The tradition that Mark was written in Rome depends on the statement of Papias that associates the gospel with Peter's martyrdom. But without the connection to Peter, the connection to Rome disappears. Internal evidence suggests that Mark's community was probably located in northern Galilee or southern Syria, perhaps in or near the villages around Caesarea Philippi. It was there, according to Mark, that Jesus was first acclaimed to be "the Christ," that is, "the Messiah" (Mark 8:27–30). But whether or not Mark can be located specifically near Caesarea Philippi, there is reason to think that it was written in or very near the Jewish homeland.

Map of probable location of Mark's community—northern Galilee or southern Syria, perhaps in or near the villages around Caesarea Philippi circa 70 C.E.

HISTORICAL CONTEXT

The year 70 was of momentous significance for Judaism and early Christianity. In that year, Jerusalem and the temple were destroyed by the Roman Empire. The destruction was the climax of a major Jewish revolt against Rome that began in the year 66.

Rome had ruled the Jewish homeland for about 130 years, beginning in 63 B.C.E. Like empires in general, Rome was politically oppressive and economically exploitative, and imposed its rule through violence and the threat of violence. Importantly, like many empires, it legitimated its rule with religious claims. Roman imperial theology not only justified its domination of the world as the will of God, but proclaimed the emperor to be divine: God, Son of God, Lord, savior of the world, and the one who brought peace on earth.

This language is very familiar to Christians, of course, but it is important to realize that it was used for the Roman Caesar before Jesus was born. Indeed, the greatest of Rome's emperors, Caesar Augustus (ruled from 31 B.C.E. to 14 C.E.) was said to have been the product of a divine conception, the son of the god Apollo and a human mother.

The Jewish revolt of 66 was thus not simply a political revolt, though it was that. It was also a rejection of Roman imperial theology and an affirmation of a Jewish theology grounded in the affirmation that the God of Israel was the true lord and Rome was not.

It was not the first Jewish revolt against Rome. Another massive revolt had occurred in 4 B.C.E. after the death of Herod the Great, the Rome-appointed ruler of the Jewish homeland, soon after Jesus was born. Rome responded with great brutality, destroying cities that refused to surrender and crucifying two thousand Jewish defenders of Jerusalem.

Now it was happening again. This time, Roman legions stationed in Syria began responding to the Jewish revolt by re-conquering Galilee in the north and then making their way south to Judea and Jerusalem. Four years later, in 70, they re-conquered Jerusalem, destroyed the city, and demolished the temple.

It was the greatest catastrophe in the history of ancient Judaism, rivaled only by the destruction of Jerusalem and its temple by the Babylonian Empire about six centuries earlier. The catastrophe was not only about devastation and death. It was intensified by the religious significance of Jerusalem's temple. According to temple theology, God was especially present in it, and God had promised to protect Jerusalem and the temple forever. In addition, the temple was the only place where sacrifices to God could be offered. But in 70, temple and sacrifice came to an end.

The war years brought massive death and suffering. Rome was not gentle. Ancient sources suggest that hundreds of thousands of Jews were killed. For Christian Jews in or near the Jewish homeland, it was a difficult time. By the Romans they were seen as Jews and risked suffering the same brutality as other Jews. And because they were committed to non-violence (as Christians were until the fourth century), they were seen by some Jews as disloyal in a time of war against a despised empire.

This is the historical interactive context of Mark. It is "a wartime gospel," to use a phrase from the scholar Daryl Schmidt.[3] The author of Mark wrote from within an early Jesus community within Judaism within the Roman Empire near the time of the great Jewish revolt and its aftermath.

Reading Mark

Mark's gospel has a simple threefold geographical pattern: Galilee, journey to Jerusalem, and Jerusalem. Mark's story of Jesus begins in Galilee, the northern part of the Jewish homeland, where most of Jesus' public activity occurs (more than half of the gospel). It climaxes with the story of Jesus' last week in Jerusalem, the traditional capital of the Jewish homeland, in the south. In between, in the middle of the gospel, is the story of Jesus' journey from Galilee to Jerusalem.

In the rest of this book, we'll explore the whole of Mark, beginning as Mark does in Galilee. Each chapter contains an overview of a section of Mark and detailed treatments of specific passages. It's a good idea to read the relevant section of Mark before reading each chapter in this book.

A concluding suggestion: if you have time, I encourage you to read all of Mark at one sitting. Relatively few people have done that. We mostly read or hear the Bible and the gospels in short segments. There is real value in experiencing the whole of a biblical book at one time. Reading Mark at a normal pace takes about two hours.

Overture and Beginning: Mark 1–3

The first three chapters of Mark not only begin the story of Jesus' public activity in Galilee but also function as an extended introduction to the gospel as a whole by introducing its central themes. To provide an overview, these chapters include:

- The overture to the gospel (1:1–20)
- A day in the public activity of Jesus (1:21–34)
- Jesus at prayer (1:35–39)
- Healing a leper (1:40–45)
- A series of conflict stories, the dominant theme of Mark 2–3

I encourage you to read Mark 1–3 before continuing.

The Overture: 1:1–20

Mark begins with an overture. So do the other gospels. Like the overture to a symphony, each sounds the central themes of the gospel that follows. In Matthew and Luke, the overtures are the stories of Jesus' birth. In John, the overture is the great "Hymn to the Word"; it opens with the famous

Overture: the opening part of a musical or literary work that sounds the central themes of the work as a whole

line, "In the beginning was the Word," now revealed and become flesh, embodied, in Jesus.

Mark's overture is quite different. There is no birth story and no hymn to the Word. Rather, Jesus appears for the first time as an adult on his way to the wilderness to be baptized by John the Baptizer in the Jordan River. There Jesus has a vision of the Spirit descending on him and hears a voice declare, "You are my son." By the time the overture ends, Jesus has begun his public activity proclaiming the coming of "the kingdom of God" and calling disciples "to follow him."

Because of the importance of Mark's overture, most of this chapter is devoted to it. I begin by quoting it in full:

[1] The beginning of the good news of Jesus Christ, the Son of God.

[2] As it is written in the prophet Isaiah,

"See, I am sending my messenger ahead of you,

who will prepare your way;

[3] the voice of one crying out in the wilderness:

'Prepare the way of the Lord, make his paths straight,'"

[4] John the baptizer appeared in the wilderness, proclaiming a baptism of repentance for the forgiveness of sins.

[5] And people from the whole Judean countryside and all the people of Jerusalem were going out to him, and were baptized by him in the river Jordan, confessing their sins.

[6] Now John was clothed with camel's hair, with a leather belt around his waist, and he ate locusts and wild honey.

[7] He proclaimed, "The one who is more powerful than I is coming after me; I am not worthy to stoop down and untie the thong of his sandals.

[8] I have baptized you with water; but he will baptize you with the Holy Spirit."

[9] In those days Jesus came from Nazareth of Galilee and was baptized by John in the Jordan.

[10] And just as he was coming up out of the water, he saw the heavens torn apart and the Spirit descending like a dove on him.

[11] And a voice came from heaven, "You are my Son, the Beloved; with you I am well pleased."

[12] And the Spirit immediately drove him out into the wilderness.

[13] He was in the wilderness forty days, tempted by Satan; and he was with the wild beasts; and the angels waited on him.

[14] Now after John was arrested, Jesus came to Galilee, proclaiming the good news of God,

[15] and saying, "The time is fulfilled, and the kingdom of God has come near; repent, and believe in the good news."

[16] As Jesus passed along the Sea of Galilee, he saw Simon and his brother Andrew casting a net into the sea, for they were fishermen.

[17] And Jesus said to them, "Follow me and I will make you fish for people." [18] And immediately they left their nets and followed him.

[19] As he went a little farther, he saw James son of Zebedee and his brother John, who were in their boat mending the nets: [20] Immediately he called them; and they left their father Zebedee in the boat with the hired men, and followed him.

Verse One: The Title

Verse one is the title of the gospel. Recall that Mark did not write "The Gospel According to Mark" at the top of his first page. Rather, this story is "*The beginning of the good news of Jesus Christ, the Son of God.*" As noted earlier, "good news" and "gospel" translate the same Greek word and we use them interchangeably.

Though brief, this verse is packed with meaning. Its first phrase, "*the beginning*" (of the good news), has at least three possible meanings. It could simply mean, "This is the beginning of this document," as when an essay might inelegantly begin, "I begin by saying. . . ." Or it could refer to the verses that soon follow narrating the appearance of John the Baptizer in the wilderness, as if Mark were saying, "The gospel of Jesus begins with John."

Or, finally, it could refer to the whole story, the whole document that follows: *all of it* is the beginning of the gospel of Jesus—a story that is not over, but that has only begun. It is not just about *past* good news, but about good news *that continues to unfold*. I suspect that Mark intends this fuller meaning: the gospel is not just about the past—it was also about Mark's present and our present.

The rest of verse one contains two of the most important early Christian affirmations about Jesus: he is "Christ" and "the Son of God." Both are "titles" of Jesus used by his followers after Easter.

"Christ" (from the Greek word *christos* that translates the Hebrew word for "messiah"—and thus Christ and Messiah are synonyms) was a term of great significance in the Jewish tradition. It meant "anointed" and, implicitly, anointed by God. In the Jewish Bible (the Christian Old Testament) the term was used to refer to the kings of Israel and Judah who were "anointed" by God (see, for example, Ps 2:2). It was also used for a foreign king, Cyrus of Persia, who in the sixth century B.C.E. permitted the Jewish exiles to return to their homeland (Isa 45:1).

By the first century, the word had acquired a more specific and exalted meaning. For many within Judaism, in diverse ways, it designated a future figure who would be anointed by God to deliver Israel from centuries of oppression. Thus in a first-century context, it is appropriate to speak not simply of *a messiah*, but of *the Messiah*. Mark affirms at the beginning of his gospel that Jesus is *the* Messiah, the hoped-for and longed-for anointed one of Israel. The good news is the story of Jesus the Messiah.

Messiah: in the OT, "God's anointed one"; by the first century, for many Jews, the hoped for deliverer of Israel

The gospel is also the story of Jesus "the Son of God." The phrase has rich meanings not only in the Jewish but also in the Roman world of Mark. In the Jewish Bible, "son of God" could refer to Israel as a whole, as in Hosea 11:1: "When Israel was a child, I loved him, and out of Egypt I called *my son*." It could also refer to a king of Israel, as in 2 Samuel 7:12–14 and Psalm 2:7. Nearer the time of Jesus, Jewish mystics were sometimes referred to as *"God's son."* What these three references have in common is that all designated a relationship of special intimacy with God.

"Son of God" was also central to Roman imperial theology. As mentioned in Chapter 1, it was one of the most important titles of the Roman emperor, beginning with Augustus Caesar who ruled the empire from 31 B.C.E. to 14 C.E. He was hailed as "the Son of God," as well as Lord and Savior of the World, the one who had brought "peace on earth"—the famous *Pax Romana*.

We will not fully understand Mark's and early Christianity's affirmation that Jesus is the Son of God unless we realize that there was another Son of God in that world. For Christians to call Jesus "the Son of God" directly countered Roman imperial theology and its rule of the world that they knew. Already in the title, Mark names the conflict that will by the end of his story lead to the execution of Jesus.

Verses Two and Three: The Way

Verses two and three of Mark's overture announce a major theme of the gospel: the good news is about "the way of the Lord." Note the threefold repetition of "way" imagery: "your way," "the way of the Lord," and "his paths."

> [2] As it is written in the prophet Isaiah, "See, I am sending my messenger ahead of you, who will prepare your way; [3] the voice of one crying out in the wilderness: 'Prepare the way of the Lord, make his paths straight.'"

The language is drawn from the Old Testament. Though Mark says all of it is from Isaiah, verse two is from Malachi 3:1. Verse three is from Isaiah 40:3.

Given the location of these verses in the narrative, they point forward to John the Baptizer. In verse four, John appears as the messenger in the wilderness who prepares the way of the Lord. As such, he is "the Forerunner" of Jesus, as he is commonly known in Eastern Christianity, whereas in Western Christianity he is most often called "the Baptist."

But the verses are not just about John—they have a much broader meaning. They name one of Mark's major themes: "the way" as a metaphor for the meaning of the gospel, the good news of Jesus Christ the Son of God.

- The importance of "the way" is indicated by Mark's frequent use of the Greek word translated into English as *the way*, and also as the *path* and *road*. In Greek, they are the same word.
- "The way" is the primary theme of the central section of Mark's gospel, as we shall see in Chapter 5. That section, 8:22–10:52, begins and ends with stories of Jesus giving sight to a blind man. In between is the story of the climactic journey of Jesus from Galilee to Jerusalem, death and resurrection. Three times in that story, Jesus solemnly speaks of his impending execution by the religious and political authorities, and after

each he speaks of *following* him—a word that belongs to the same metaphorical family as *the way, path,* and *road.*

■ At the end of that section, Mark tells us that the blind man who has just been healed "*followed [Jesus] on the way*" (10:52). To regain sight, to see again, means to follow Jesus on the way. In the next verse, Jesus and those following him arrive in Jerusalem, the destination of the way.

■ The cumulative meaning of Mark's central section: to follow Jesus is to follow him on the way that leads to Jerusalem, the place of confrontation with the authorities, death, and resurrection. For Mark, this is the way that Jesus taught, embodied, and called his followers to follow.

As a metaphor for how to live, "the way" is central to both the Old Testament and New Testament. The Jewish Bible often speaks of contrasting ways: "the way of life" and "the way of death"; "the wise way" and "the foolish way." So does Jesus, who also speaks of "the broad way" and the "narrow way." In John 14:6, Jesus himself is "the way"— he embodies it, incarnates it, in his life, death, and resurrection. According to the book of Acts, the earliest name of the post-Easter movement was "the Way" (9:2).

As an image for the religious life, "the way" is quite different from common modern understandings of what it means to be Christian. Many Protestants as well as some Catholics think that the Christian life is foundationally about *believing*, understood as believing a set of statements about the Bible and God and Jesus. And, of course, an effort at good behavior is also included.

But the gospel as "the way of Jesus" suggests a path and a person to be followed, and not primarily a set of beliefs to be believed. Verses two and three are not simply Mark's introduction to John the Baptizer. Rather, they sound the theme of Jesus as "the way of the Lord"—and he calls people to follow *the way* that he taught and that Mark saw revealed in him.

Verses Four through Eight: John the Baptizer

Mark's overture now introduces John the Baptizer and concisely narrates his activity and message. John was of great significance to early

Christians as they told the story of Jesus. All four gospels and the book of Acts begin the story of the adult Jesus with John. Moreover, John was significant enough that the first-century Jewish historian Josephus also refers to him.

He was a strange figure, even by the conventions of his time. He wore animal skins ("camel's hair"), ate locusts and wild honey, and preached "in the wilderness." He was what scholars call "a popular prophet" in a twofold sense: not an "official" prophet, but "of the people," and popular in the sense of attracting a following. Indeed, John became widely enough known to attract the attention of Herod Antipas, son of Herod the Great and ruler of Galilee who, as we learn later in Mark, arrested and executed him.

Immersion in water—baptism—was a common Jewish religious practice. There were two different kinds, differentiated by frequency and function. Some ritual immersions were repeated again and again as prescribed by Jewish law—for example, after a woman's menstrual period, or a man's nocturnal emission. This is immersion as a purification ritual. The second kind was a once-only ritual of conversion. Namely, when a Gentile converted to Judaism, the process included immersion. This is baptism as a ritual of initiation into a new life.

John's baptism was more like the second than the first. It was not a repeated ritual of purification. Yet it also differed from the second in important respects. John's baptism was for Jews, not for Gentile converts to Judaism. It was, as Matthew and Luke say, for the "children of Abraham."

Its meaning is suggested by its location. That John baptized in the Jordan River and not just anyplace is significant. The Jordan was the traditional boundary between "the wilderness" and "the promised land." It was through the Jordan that the Israelites had passed to enter the promised land at the climax of the story of the exodus from Egypt more than a thousand years earlier. The wilderness and the Jordan were also associated with the Jewish experience of exile. It was through the wilderness separating Babylon from the homeland that the exiles journeyed in order to return. Thus John's baptism resonated with images of exodus and exile and "the way" that leads from bondage to liberation and from exile to return.

Mark 1:9–11: Baptism, Vision, and Voice

BAPTISM

In verse nine, Jesus appears for the first time in Mark's narrative as he travels from Nazareth to be baptized by John. Mark does not tell us Jesus' motive. But he had to be more than curious about what he had heard about John. Why else would he walk several days from Nazareth—perhaps as far as a hundred miles—to where John was baptizing? For the same reason, we must also imagine that Jesus spent some time with John rather than going for a quick baptism and a journey home a few days later. We should probably think of John as Jesus' mentor.

It is instructive to compare Mark's story of the baptism with Matthew's. To Mark's account, Matthew adds a conversation between Jesus and John (3:14–15). John recognizes Jesus as his superior: John says, "I need to be baptized by you, and do you come to me?" The effect is to suggest that Jesus didn't need to be baptized by John, but nevertheless agreed to be.

But in Mark there is no hint that John recognized Jesus as superior to him, or that Jesus accepted baptism in spite of that. Rather, Mark's account suggests that Jesus' decision to be baptized indicates an acceptance of John's call to repentance and an identification with John's message and vision—in short, that Jesus was, for at least a while, one of John's disciples.

VISION AND VOICE

Verses 10–11 report that Jesus had a vision and heard a voice at his baptism: "He *saw* the heavens torn apart and the Spirit descending like a dove on him. And *a voice* came from heaven, 'You are my Son, the Beloved; with you I am well pleased.'" The language echoes phrases from the Old Testament, especially the prophets Ezekiel and Isaiah.

Audition: the auditory equivalent of a vision

Visions are a dramatic kind of religious experience. Reported in many religions, they involve an ecstatic state of consciousness in which something "beyond" the ordinary is "seen," as the word "vision" suggests. They are often accompanied by a voice, an "audition," to use a semi-technical term. Vision and audition frequently go together. What is seen and heard has sacred significance and is often life-changing.

They are important in the Bible and associated with its major figures: in the Old Testament, Abraham, Jacob, Moses, and many prophets experienced visions; in the New Testament, Jesus, Paul, Peter, the author of Revelation, and others did. Moreover, they are commonly about vocation—being called by God to a specific task.

Visions fall into two primary categories. Some involve seeing into another level or layer of reality, another "world." For example, Ezekiel saw the heavens opened and visions of God (1:1). Isaiah "saw the Lord sitting on a throne, high and lofty," attended by six-winged creatures from another world, accompanied by an audition that called him to his prophetic vocation (6:1–13).

Some visions involve seeing an ordinary object in this world but transfigured and suffused with sacred significance. In Exodus 3, Moses saw a bush that burned without being consumed, filled with the fiery radiance of God. Then a voice spoke to him, commissioning him to be the liberator of Israel. Jeremiah's visions and call to be a prophet included an almond branch and a boiling pot (1:11–13).

Jesus' baptismal vision and audition belong to the first category. As Mark presents this experience:

- Jesus saw the heavens torn apart, the heavens open, and the Spirit descending upon him. The affirmation that Jesus was anointed by the Spirit is central not only to Mark but to the other gospels as well. In Luke, Jesus' "inaugural address" begins: "The Spirit of the Lord is upon me . . . he has anointed me to bring good news to the poor" (4:18).
- Jesus hears "a voice from heaven." It is, of course, the voice of God. In Judaism, such a voice was called in Hebrew a *bath qol,* which means literally "the daughter of a sound." The phrase is evocative and provocative, like the words used to describe the prophet Elijah's experience of the voice of God: he heard "a sound of sheer silence" (1 Kings 19:12). This is no ordinary sound.

  Bath qol: "the daughter of a sound"

- Jesus hears the voice say to him: "You are my Son." As part of Mark's overture, the voice repeats and underlines the status given to Jesus in the title of the gospel: "Son of God."

Mark presents all of this as a private experience of Jesus. It is instructive to compare Mark to Matthew and Luke, both of whom used Mark as a source as they wrote their gospels. In Mark 1:11, the voice addresses Jesus in the second person singular: "*You* are my Son." In Matthew 3:17, the voice is not addressed to Jesus, but is a third-person declaration (to the crowd?) about Jesus: "*This* is my Son." Luke 3:22 may also "objectify" the experience: the Spirit descends *in bodily form* like a dove, perhaps implying that anybody there would have seen it.

But in Mark, only Jesus sees the vision and hears the voice. They are an internal experience, not a public event and disclosure. This is consistent with Mark's gospel as a whole: in Mark, Jesus' status as Son of God is not part of Jesus' message. Indeed, in Mark, the first human to declare Jesus to be the Son of God does so at the crucifixion, at the end of Jesus' historical life.

That Mark presents Jesus' vision and audition as a private, internal experience does not in any way diminish its significance. For Mark, it is vitally important: the story of Jesus begins with a dramatic experience of the sacred. Like other great figures in the Jewish tradition, Jesus had a vision and heard the voice of God calling him to his vocation.

Mark 1:12–13: Tempted/Tested in the Wilderness

The overture continues. The Spirit that descended on Jesus at his baptism *immediately* (one of Mark's favorite words) "drove Jesus out into the wilderness." There he spent "forty days" and was "tempted (or 'tested') by Satan." Abruptly, the story ends: "And Jesus was with the wild beasts; and the angels waited on him."

The account is very brief compared to the longer and more familiar story of the tempting/testing of Jesus in Matthew 4:1–11 and Luke 4:1–13. In those accounts, we are told that Jesus *fasted* for forty days. Then "the devil" (as Matthew and Luke name him) appears and presents Jesus with three temptations: to turn stones into bread, to jump from a high place and trust God to rescue him, and to worship Satan in exchange for all the kingdoms of this world. Perhaps we might think of these as the materialist, sensationalist, and imperialist temptations.

But Mark does not specify the temptations: he simply tells us that Jesus was "tempted/tested by Satan." Even so, because Mark's account immediately follows the vision in which Jesus is told that he is God's Son, it is reasonable to presume that the temptation concerned the question, "What does it mean to be Son of God and God's beloved? What is this role and identity about?"

Mark 1:14–15: The Kingdom of God

All of Mark's overture is important, but these verses are particularly so. They indicate the beginning of Jesus' public activity and name the content of his message, his gospel.

Verse 14 "dates" the beginning of Jesus' public activity to the arrest of John by Herod Antipas: *"Now after John was arrested, Jesus came to Galilee"*—presumably from the wilderness where he had been with John—*"proclaiming the good news (gospel) of God."* The importance of John for Jesus is underlined. Only after John had been arrested did Jesus begin proclaiming "the gospel of God."

Verse 15 tells us what the gospel of God is. For Mark, it is Jesus' "inaugural address," the first time Jesus speaks. Like the inaugural scenes of the public activity of Jesus in the other gospels, it is an advance summary of what the gospel, the good news, is about. In Mark, Jesus' first words are, "The time is fulfilled, and *the kingdom of God has come near*; repent, and believe in *the good news.*"

THE KINGDOM OF GOD

The good news—the gospel—is about "the kingdom of God." Before continuing, I suggest a reflection exercise. If you were asked to state the gospel, the heart of the Christian message, in a sentence or two, what would you say? If you grew up Christian, what would you have said at the end of childhood—around age twelve or so? And how would you answer now? Pretty much the same, or very different?

Our answer is important, for it decisively shapes what we think the Christian life is about. As I recall how I would have answered the question at the end of my childhood, I would have said that the gospel—the Christian good news—in a sentence is that Jesus died for our sins so that we can be forgiven and go to heaven, provided that we believe this. Note the emphasis on sin, forgiveness, the after-life, and believing. I no longer think of this as "the gospel," even as I am also aware that a good number of Christians do—consciously or unconsciously, insistently or uncertainly.

But this is not Mark's understanding of "the good news," the gospel. Rather, for Mark (and for Matthew and Luke as well), the gospel is about "the kingdom of God." This is also a consensus within scholarship. Several decades ago a New Testament scholar wrote: if you asked a hundred experts on the gospels from around the world what was most central to the message, the gospel, of Jesus, all of them—whether Catholic, Protestant, Jewish, or non-believer—would say, "the kingdom of God."

So: what is "the kingdom of God"? What did this phrase mean in the first-century context of Mark, Jesus, and early Christianity?

- The kingdom of God is not about life after death, but about life in this world. This statement does not deny an afterlife, but emphasizes that the kingdom of God is *for the earth*. Christians should not be surprised by this. Every time we pray the Lord's Prayer, we pray "Your kingdom come *on earth*" as it already is in heaven. As the contemporary scholar John Dominic Crossan says, heaven's in great shape—earth is where the problems are.

Kingdom of God: God's "dream" for the earth: a world of justice and peace

- Kingdom of God was a political as well as religious metaphor in the first century. As a political metaphor, kingdom was the most common form of political organization in that world. Mark's and Jesus' hearers knew about the kingdom of Herod and the kingdom of Rome; thus the *kingdom* of God would have suggested a kingdom different from the kingdoms of Herod and Rome. As a religious metaphor, it referred to the kingdom *of God*—it was about allegiance to the God of Israel and what life would be like on earth if God were king and the rulers of this world were not.
- The kingdom of God is about the transformation of life in this world—of individual lives and of the world itself. It is "the

dream of God" for the earth, to echo the title of a recent book.[4] Grounded in the Jewish Bible, God's dream—God's will, God's passion—is a transformed world. The two main features of God's dream are justice and peace. Justice means distributive justice— everybody should have enough of God's earth, not as the result of charity but as the product of justice, namely, the way the world is put together. The other primary feature is peace—a world in which to echo Isaiah and Micah, the instruments of war become implements of agriculture: the nations shall beat their swords into plowshares and their spears into pruning hooks, and nation shall not make war against nation anymore (Isa 2:4, Mic 4:1–4).

> **Distributive justice:** the concept that everybody should have enough of God's earth, not as the result of charity but as the product of justice

Though the phrase "the kingdom of God" is relatively unusual within first-century Judaism, it named what many Jews longed and hoped for: a world in which God is king and the rulers—the domination systems—of this world are not; a world in which oppressive and exploitative systems enforced by power and violence are no more; a world in which the poverty and misery, malnourishment and desperation, premature death and wars created by them are no more. To use language from Micah 4:1–4 again, it would be a world in which people lived in peace and in which every family had its own vine and fig tree, its own source of sustenance. In such a world—a world of justice and peace—the powerful closing words of the passage proclaim: "And no one shall make them afraid."

Most Jews shared this hope. The exception was some (perhaps many) of the wealthy and powerful—the ruling elite, as they are often called. These included a small aristocracy, other people of wealth (including some *nouveau riche*), and senior officials in the court of Herod and in the temple in Jerusalem. They did well within the present system, and thus naturally were less-disposed to yearn for change. But even with their extended families included, they were still a very small percentage of the population.

Yet there were different beliefs among Jews about how this transformed world would come about. Some believed that only God could do it—and they hoped that God would do so soon. Some thought that observing God's laws with great faithfulness could hasten the time of its coming. Some thought that passion for the transformation of God's world required a war of revolt against Rome and that God would aid the effort.

Some thought God would bring about the new world through a human figure—the Messiah. A few thought there would be two Messiahs—one priestly, the other royal. Some thought God would accomplish this transformed world without a human intermediary. And no doubt many hoped for a world transformed by God without having precise convictions about how God would do it.

Thus when Mark crystallizes Jesus' message of "the kingdom of God," he is naming God's dream and Israel's hope for a different kind of world *on earth*, to echo the Lord's Prayer once again. The kingdom of God, Mark says in his overture, is the heart of the gospel.

The Kingdom Is Near

In Jesus' inaugural address in Mark, he not only names the gospel as the kingdom of God, but also says it "*has come near.*" What does this mean? The Greek verb is notoriously difficult to translate because of its ambiguity.

It could mean "near in time": the kingdom will *soon* be here, but it isn't yet. The Greek verb could also mean "has come"—it is already here. But "near" can also refer not primarily to proximity in time, but to accessibility: the kingdom is near, at hand, here, in the sense that it is beginning and available—and one can enter it now. It can mean becoming involved in a process and not simply waiting for God to do it soon. Which of these meanings the Jesus of Mark intends will become clearer as the gospel unfolds.

Repent and Believe

There is one more phrase in the inaugural address of Jesus in Mark's overture. After the proclamation, "The kingdom of God has come near," Jesus says, "Repent, and believe in the good news."

We begin with the meaning of "repent." Its biblical meaning is quite different from a common Christian meaning. For many (and for me when I was young), repentance is associated primarily with sin and forgiveness. It means being sorry for our sins, confessing them, resolving not to continue committing them, and then, as a result, receiving God's forgiveness.

But this is not the meaning of "repent" in the Bible, in the gospel of Mark, and in the gospel of Jesus. There, its resonances—its meanings—are twofold. One comes from the linguistic home of the word in biblical Hebrew. It is associated primarily with the Jewish experience of exile. To repent means "to return"—to journey on *the way* of return to God from a place of exile. Its Greek roots—the language of Mark and the New Testament—mean *to go beyond the mind that you have.* The mind that we have is shaped by culture and convention. The mind that we are to have is one shaped by God and the dream of God. To repent is to embark on the way of return to God by going beyond the mind that we have.

> **Repent:** in Biblical terminology, to "return" or to "go beyond the mind that you have," not necessarily to ask for forgiveness

We continue with the meaning of the verb "believe"—to believe in the good news, the gospel. In the ancient world of the Bible and in Christianity until around the year 1600, "to believe" did not mean accepting a set of statements to be true; it did not mean believing in a list of beliefs. Rather, "to believe" meant to commit oneself, to give oneself, to a relationship marked by loyalty, allegiance, and commitment. "To believe" in "the good news" that the kingdom had come near was to commit one's self to God and God's kingdom and its vision of a very different kind of world.

This, Mark says in his overture, is the gospel of God, the gospel of Jesus. It is about the kingdom of God, its nearness, and the call to return to God by going beyond the minds that we have.

MARK 1:16–20: THE CALL TO FOLLOW JESUS

Mark's overture concludes with the call of Jesus' first four disciples: Simon (Peter), his brother Andrew, and James and John, the sons of Zebedee. They are called to follow Jesus. Indeed the verb "follow" occurs three times in these verses and it belongs to the metaphor of "the way." As the overture ends, Mark's language connects back to "the way of the Lord" in Mark 1:2–3. To follow Jesus is to follow "the way of the Lord"—and that way is about the kingdom of God.

Beyond the Overture: The Rest of Mark 1–3

Mark 1:21–3:35 continues the task of introducing the central themes of the gospel as a whole. We see Jesus teaching, casting out demons, healing, praying, associating with "unclean" and outcast people, calling more disciples, and attracting crowds. All of these are important throughout the gospel. This section also introduces the theme of conflict: Mark 2–3 are dominated by a series of conflict stories that anticipate the conflict that will dominate the last chapters of the gospel. Already the shadow of the cross casts itself upon Mark's story of Jesus.

MARK 1:21–45

Immediately following the overture, the events related in verses 1:21–34 all occur on a single day. Note that this passage begins on a Sabbath (verse 21) and ends "that evening at sundown" (verse 32). Moreover, in Mark, it is the first day of Jesus' public activity. Perhaps Mark means to suggest that this was what an ordinary day with Jesus was like.

The day begins with Jesus and his four disciples going to the synagogue in Capernaum, a fishing village on the north shore of the Sea of Galilee. Then:

- Jesus teaches "with authority" and not as "one of the scribes."
- He casts out a demon from a possessed man.
- He heals Simon's (Peter's) mother-in-law of a fever.
- In the evening, as Sabbath ends, he heals "many who were sick or possessed with demons."

These activities on the first day—teaching, exorcism, and healing—are central to the rest of Mark's story of Jesus.

Chapter one concludes with two short texts:

- Jesus prays (1:35–39). That Mark includes this in his first chapter indicates that he saw prayer as central to who Jesus was. The combination of solitude and duration in the details of the text suggest a form of contemplative prayer: early in the morning while it was still dark, Jesus went out to a deserted place in order to pray. The text suggests he was there for a long time—his disciples had to hunt for him.

■ Jesus heals a leper (1:40–45). Lepers were among "the unclean." Jesus heals him and thus makes him "clean" and tells him to present himself before the official adjudicators of clean/unclean, pure/impure. The fame of Jesus spreads.

CHAPTERS TWO AND THREE

Mark's second and third chapters are dominated by conflict stories. They announce the theme of conflict that will, by the end of the gospel, lead to Jesus' execution. Here are some of the conflicts Jesus becomes embroiled in during these chapters:

■ 2:1–12. *Conflict about Jesus' authority to forgive.* Jesus pronounces forgiveness to a paralyzed man and releases him from his paralysis. Protest comes from "scribes" (a literate class whose task was biblical interpretation).

■ 2:13–17. *Conflict about Jesus' inclusive meal practice.* Jesus eats with "tax collectors and sinners," designations for marginalized and outcast Jews. Protest comes from "the scribes of the Pharisees," a Jewish group committed to intensified standards of purity and separation from all that was "impure" or "unclean."

■ 2:18–22. *Conflict about religious practices.* The conflict is about fasting: disciples of John the Baptizer and the Pharisees protest that Jesus and his disciples do not fast as they do.

■ 2:23–28. *Conflict about Sabbath observance.* The protestors are Pharisees.

■ 3:1–6. *Conflict about Sabbath continues.* Prompted by Jesus healing a man *on the Sabbath*, Pharisees and Herodians (a group loyal to Herod Antipas, who arrested and executed John) protest. The conflict becomes deadly: they conspire about how to destroy Jesus.

■ 3:7–19. *An interlude in the conflict theme:* Jesus' reputation grows and he calls eight more disciples in addition to the first four.

■ 3:20–21. *Conflict between Jesus and his family:* Members of Jesus' family eek to restrain him because they think "he has gone out of his mind." We should be surprised by this. It was too much for Matthew and Luke; both omit these verses. But Mark reports that Jesus' family (later in verse 31 named as "his mother and his brothers") thought Jesus was "out of his mind"—crazy, insane, alarmingly abnormal, whatever words best express this. There was something, readers must conclude, very different about Jesus.

- 3:22–30. *Conflict with "scribes who came down from Jerusalem."* They accuse Jesus of being possessed by "Beelzebul, the ruler of the demons." The issue for them and for Jesus' family is the same: what's gotten into Jesus—what kind of spirit does he have? Is he crazy? Or in league with the devil and possessed by a demonic spirit?

The section continues with Jesus affirming that the Spirit in him cannot be in league with the devil, for it is destroying Satan's kingdom and plundering the house of the strong man (a metaphor for Satan).

The section concludes with a verse that speaks of the unforgivable sin and names it as blasphemy against the Holy Spirit. The verse has terrified many Christians, including many in my generation: I can remember scary conversations about what the unforgivable sin is. In Mark's context, its meaning is clear: if you do not perceive the presence of God's Spirit in Jesus, if you think whatever was in him came from somewhere else, your life will not change. This passage is not about how to get into heaven. Rather, not discerning the Spirit in Jesus is to stay the way you are and to fail to participate in the dream of God.

- 3:31–35. *More conflict with Jesus' family.* His family seeks him out again. When told of their presence, Jesus says, "Who are my mother and my brothers?" Then, looking at those who sat around him: "Here are my mother and my brothers. Whoever does the will of God is my brother and sister and mother." Clearly, the family of Jesus transcends blood relationships.

In these conflict stories, Mark announces the major theme of his gospel: Jesus' passion for the kingdom of God will lead to a final and fatal conflict with the authorities who ruled his world. The second and third chapters of Mark anticipate the cross.

CHAPTER TWO

Parables and Miracles: Mark 4–5

Mark 4 and 5 continue the story of Jesus' activity in Galilee, focusing on two themes: first, Jesus as a teacher who instructs in parables, and second, as a performer of mighty deeds. He stills a storm on the sea, performs a dramatic exorcism, and heals two women. It's a good idea to read Mark 2 and 3 before turning to this chapter.

Most of chapter four (verses 1–34) treats the first theme. We are told that Jesus commonly taught in parables, and then a series of parables about sowing and seeds follows.

- A sower sows seeds that fall on different kinds of ground (4:1–9, followed by commentary in 4:10–20)
- The kingdom of God is like a growing seed (4:26–29)
- The kingdom of God is like a mustard seed (4:30–32)

The second theme—mighty deeds, commonly called "miracle stories"—begins near the end of chapter four and continues through chapter five.

- Jesus stills a storm on the sea and saves his disciples (4:35–41)

- Jesus casts a host of unclean spirits out of a demoniac whose name is Legion; the demons enter a herd of pigs that rush into the sea and drown (5:1–20)
- Jairus, a synagogue leader, begs Jesus to heal his twelve-year-old daughter who is near death (5:21–24)
- On the way to Jairus' house, Jesus heals a woman who had a flow of blood for twelve years (5:25–34)
- Jesus is told that Jairus' daughter has died, but continues to their home anyway, where he declares that the girl "is not dead but sleeping" and restores her to normal life (5:35–43)

We focus on several texts from these chapters: the parable of the sower, the story of Jesus stilling a storm, and the story of the exorcism of "Legion." We will conclude with stories of Jesus healing two women.

Jesus Taught in Parables

At the beginning of the collection of parables in chapter four, Mark tells us that Jesus typically taught in parables. The *NRSV*, the biblical translation used in this book unless otherwise noted, reads:

> Again he began to teach beside the sea. Such a very large crowd gathered around him that he got into a boat on the sea and sat there, while the whole crowd was beside the sea on the land. He began to teach them many things in parables and in his teaching he said to them. . . . (Mark 4:1–2)

Later in the chapter, we are told that Jesus "did not speak to them (the crowd) except in parables" (4:34).

That Mark is describing continuing and typical behavior is even clearer in the *Scholars Version* translation of the Bible. This version is in one sense more literal than the *NRSV*: it preserves the shift in verb tenses of Mark's Greek—from past to present to a tense that indicates continuing activity.

> Once again he started to teach beside the sea. [Now Mark shifts to present tense; note how vivid and immediate the narration becomes.] An enormous crowd gathers around him, so he climbs into a boat and sits there on the water facing the huge crowd on the shore. [Now Mark shifts to a Greek tense, indicating continuing and typical action.] He would then teach them many things in parables. In the course of his teaching he would tell them. . . .

In short, Mark does not mean that on this one occasion, Jesus taught in parables, or taught these parables in particular on that occasion. Rather, this scene narrates how Jesus commonly taught: he taught in parables.

Parable: a story that invites hearers to see something they might not otherwise see

Mark's statement is confirmed by Matthew and Luke (who include a large number of parables not found in Mark) and affirmed by scholars. Parables, along with aphorisms, which are short memorable and provocative sayings, were Jesus' most common form of teaching.

Aphorism: short memorable and provocative saying

Scholars differ on how many parables there are in the gospels, depending upon how "parable" is defined, but most speak of thirty to forty. Whatever the number, more parables are attributed to Jesus than to any other ancient Jewish teacher. Using parables was characteristic of his style of teaching.

It is instructive to think about what a parable is.

- *First, parables are stories—something happens in a parable.* They are narratives. This is true even for very brief parables such as the stories of a man finding treasure in a field (Matt 13:44) and a merchant in search of fine pearls (Matt 13:45). The story form is even clearer in longer parables, such as the stories of the Prodigal Son, the Good Samaritan, the Workers in the Vineyard (Luke 15:11–32; Luke 10:29–37; Matt 20:1–16), and a parable later in Mark, the Wicked Tenants of the Vineyard (12:1–9).
- *Second, parables are made-up stories.* They are not factual—their purpose is not to report something that really occurred. And yet they are important. They matter. They are meaningful and meaning-filled, truthful and truth-filled. Their truth does not depend on their factuality; rather they are about meaning, insight, seeing. They are invitations to see something that you might not otherwise see.
- *Third, parables were oft-repeated.* Jesus would have told each of his parables many times. He was an itinerant and oral teacher, not a sedentary writer of documents. An itinerant oral teacher uses a good story (and a striking aphorism) frequently. What

a waste it would be to use a story like the Prodigal Son or the Good Samaritan, or an aphorism like "Leave the dead to bury the dead," only once.

So what we have in the parables of Jesus is "the gist" of stories that he told often at varying lengths and with different incidental details. For example, the story of the Prodigal Son in Luke 15:11–32, the longest parable, takes three to four minutes to read aloud at a reasonable pace. Yet it is easy to imagine a gifted storyteller like Jesus expanding this parable to twenty minutes or more.

- *Fourth, the purpose of parables is to initiate thought by inviting the hearer of the parable into the story*. People who hear parables are impelled to ask themselves what the story is all about. It is easy to imagine that when Jesus taught in parables, he left time for audience response and interaction. Indeed, given that he was an oral teacher, it's hard to imagine otherwise. Can you picture a crowd listening silently and respectfully to a parable of Jesus, and then walking off in silence by themselves to think about what it might mean? Probably not. Parables presume and invite conversation.
- *Fifth, some parables describe exceptional behavior, and others ordinary actions*. Some parables are surprising: a father lavishly welcomes home his wayward wastrel son; a despised Samaritan stops to help a Jew after a priest and Levite passed by; a vineyard owner pays all his workers the same whether they have labored the whole day or only an hour. Here the focus is on thinking about the surprise.

Some parables, though, are stories of things that typically happen—a woman puts yeast into flour as she makes bread, a shepherd searches for a lost sheep, a woman looks for a coin she has lost. When typical behavior is described, the parable raises the question: yes, that's what people do—but what is this story about? What does it mean?

The Parable of the Sower: 4:3–9

The parable of the sower describes typical behavior. He sows as sowers did in that world, "broadcasting" seeds by moving his arm in an arc while releasing a stream of seeds from his hand. The result is what happens when sowing is done this way: the seeds fell on different kinds of ground. Some fell on a path, and birds ate them because they could not germinate in the hard-packed earth. Some fell on rocky ground where the soil was thin—though the seeds germinated, they soon withered. Some fell among thorns, and the thorns choked them. Finally, some "fell into good soil and brought forth grain, growing up and increasing and yielding thirty and sixty and a hundredfold." The parable concludes: "Let anyone with ears to hear listen!"

There is nothing surprising here. None of Jesus' listeners would have had to debate whether this is what happens, as some might want to debate whether the father of the prodigal son behaved responsibly, or whether a Samaritan could ever be a good guy. This parable would draw the response, "Yes, that's what happens. And so?" The question becomes, "What is this parable about?"

Mark provides an explanation in verses 13–20. This is unusual—parables in the gospels are not commonly explained. These verses, however, treat the parable as if it were an allegory: the seed is "the word" and the different kinds of ground are different kinds of people, or different ways that people receive "the word."

Scholars disagree about whether the explanation goes back to Jesus. Most see it as created by Mark or a predecessor.

Allegory: a story in which most of the details represent something else

For a moment, let us set aside Mark's explanation and try to imagine from the parable itself what it meant in the context of Mark's portrait of Jesus as proclaimer of the kingdom of God. For this is the message of Jesus according to his inaugural address in Mark 1:15.

We begin with the seed. Mark's explanation that the seed is "the word" is reasonable. But what is "the word"? Because of its associations among Christians, "the word" is often thought to refer in a generalized way to preaching "the Word of God."

But given Jesus' inaugural speech in which he identified the kingdom of God as the heart of his gospel, "seed" as "word" is likely to have a more specific meaning—it is the word *of the kingdom.* Interestingly, this is how Matthew understood it (Matt. 13:19).

Moreover, seed/word as the gospel of the kingdom is supported by the other two parables in Mark 4. Both are about sowing and seeds and both are explicitly said to be about the kingdom of God (4:26–29 and 4:30–32). This, Mark says, is what Jesus was doing: sowing the kingdom.

As a parable about what happens to the message of the kingdom, this story could have any (and perhaps all) of the following meanings. It does not matter whether Mark intended all of them, for the meanings of parables and other stories are not limited to the conscious intention of the author. They can have multiple meanings.

- The parable could explain why only a relative few have responded to the message of the kingdom. Only some hearts are fertile.
- The parable could provide encouragement to "keep on sowing" the seed of the kingdom. Although some seed will land on infertile ground, some will thrive and multiply. You never know which is which.
- The parable could offer counsel in the face of discouragement. This is like the interpretation above with an additional nuance: don't be discouraged—keep on keeping on.
- The parable raises a question in the mind of the hearers: what kind of ground, or soil, are we? Do we hear and respond to the word of the kingdom differently because of the kind of soil we are? And is it possible to become a different kind of soil?

Some of these meanings explain why some scholars have suggested that the parable should be called "The Parable of the Soils" and not "The Parable of the Sower." The different kinds of ground do receive as much—perhaps more—emphasis as the sower. Yet there is value in both titles, for the parable is about *both*: the sowing of the kingdom and the way the kingdom is received by people who hear about it.

Mark's section on parables concludes in 4:33–34. Mark 4:35–41, the story of Jesus stilling the sea, and all of Mark 5 narrate a series of miracle stories. An important note: chapter divisions were not added to the New Testament until about a thousand years after it was written, and verse divisions about a century after that. Thus chapter divisions in the gospels are not based on how those who wrote the documents divided their material. Sometimes the divisions divide material that should be kept together. So it is here: Mark 4:35–41 belongs with Mark 5 more than it does with the earlier part of Mark 4 on parables. Of course, all of Mark belongs together— but sometimes our chapter divisions obscure the way smaller blocks of material are connected.

Jesus Stills the Sea: 4:35–41

This is the first "nature miracle" in Mark. To explain the phrase, scholars commonly divide the stories of Jesus' spectacular deeds into two main categories. The first is stories of healings and exorcisms. Most scholars, whether Christian or not, affirm that the tradition that Jesus was a healer and exorcist is based on historical memory. Indeed, more stories are told about Jesus as a healer and exorcist than about any other figure in the Jewish tradition. To affirm that these stories are based on memory does not mean that they are factually exact and precise accounts. But it does mean that they are based on memory even as the way they are told most often—maybe even always—gives them a more-than-factual, metaphorical, meaning as well.

Already in chapters 1–3, Mark has told us one exorcism story (1:21–26) and four healing stories (1:29–31, 40–45; 2:1–12; 3:1–6), plus summary statements that Jesus healed many and cast demons out of many (1:32–34, 39; 3:10–12).

The second category, nature miracles, consists of stories in which the non-human world is affected. These include stories of Jesus stilling the sea, multiplying a few loaves and fish to feed a large crowd, and, in the gospel of John, changing water into wine at a wedding feast. The verdict on the factuality of these stories is different, in part because of their spectacular character.

FACTUALITY AND THE NATURE MIRACLES

So we pause to reflect about the question of factuality and whether it matters. The question has two components. First, are the nature miracles stories meant to be factual reports? Is this how we are to understand them? And if they are intended to be factual, are they true? Did these things happen? Do things like this ever happen? And regardless of how spectacular the stories are, are we nevertheless to believe that Jesus did these things—indeed, that believing them is one of the meanings of faith? Some, perhaps many, Christians would say so. And for some, their factuality matters very much—these miracles "prove" that Jesus really was the Son of God and divine. Only a divine being could do such things.

The second component of the question is quite different: Is the factuality of these stories important to their meaning and truthfulness? Does their importance depend on their factuality? If they're not factual, are they then untrue—either mistaken reports or pious fabrications? Or is there another way of understanding them?

AS PARABOLIC NARRATIVES

There is a third way of understanding these stories. They are what I called in the Introduction "metaphorical narratives." In this chapter, I suggest that we think of them as "parabolic narratives," by which I mean the same thing.

The model for seeing them this way is the parables of Jesus. Recall from the first part of this chapter that Jesus' parables are not factual stories, and yet all Christians agree that they matter—that they are meaning-filled and truth-filled, even though Jesus made them up.

Just as the parables of Jesus are meaningful and truthful even though he made them up, so also the stories of the nature miracles are meaningful and truthful even if his followers made them up. Jesus told parables about God; his followers may well have told parables about Jesus.

This option moves beyond the question of factuality. It rejects the limited twofold choice of "they happened" or "they're not true." Note that hearing them as parabolic narratives does not insist that they did not happen. Rather, it affirms that that is the wrong question to focus on. It would be like getting into a heated argument about whether there really was a prodigal son or a good Samaritan. Doing so would miss the point of these parables. So also a parabolic approach to the nature miracle stories says, in effect: believe whatever you want about whether they happened the way they are told—now let's talk about what these stories mean.

The Sea

Mark 4:35–41 is the first of two stories in Mark that speak about Jesus having mastery over the sea. In this one, Jesus stills a storm that threatens to overwhelm his disciples. In the second, Mark 6:47–52, Jesus does the same and also walks on water.

That this story is set on "the sea" is significant. Within Mark's narrative, "the sea" is the Sea of Galilee, even though calling this body of water a sea is a bit of misnomer. It is in fact a fresh-water lake, and a not especially big one, about twelve miles long and seven miles wide. Luke 8:22–23 more accurately calls it a "lake."

But "the sea" in Mark's story is more than the Sea of Galilee. In the Jewish context in which Mark was immersed (and Jesus and earliest Christianity), "the sea" had metaphorical meanings.

In the Old Testament, "the sea" often has a more-than-literal meaning. In Genesis 1, it is the primordial chaos preceding creation. While the earth was still void and without form, "darkness covered the face of the deep," the sea. Then God's spirit (or breath or wind—they are the same word in Hebrew) "swept over the face of the waters." The first act of creation follows. But the deep, the waters, the sea, was the primordial force that God put in order.

In the rest of the Old Testament, the sea continues to have this more-than-literal meaning. It was the home of ancient sea monsters named as Leviathan (Ps 74:14, 74:13–14; Job 41:1–34) and Rahab (Ps 89:9–10, Isa 51:9–10). In the story of the exodus, God parted the sea so that the Israelites could pass to safety as they were pursued by the army of Pharaoh.

Ancient Israel praised God by proclaiming God's mastery of the sea. Psalm 95:5 exclaims: the sea is God's, for God made it! In Job 38, the voice of God from the whirlwind emphasizes God's power over the sea:

> Who shut in the sea with doors when it burst out from the womb?—when I made the clouds its garments and thick darkness its swaddling band, and prescribed bounds for it, and set bars and doors, and said, "Thus far shall you come and no farther, and here shall your proud waves be stopped"? (Job 38:8–11)

Psalm 107 praises God's mastery over the sea in language that resembles Mark's story of Jesus stilling a storm. It begins by extolling

God for delivering those who wandered in the desert wilderness, hungry and thirsty (verses 4–9); those who sat in darkness, gloom and bondage (verses 10–16); those who were sick in their sinful ways (verses 17–22). Then, in verse 23 we are told about people at sea in a storm. As the waves mounted up to heaven and descended to the depths, "Their courage melted away in their calamity; they reeled and staggered like drunkards, and were at their wits' end."

> Then they cried to the Lord in their trouble, and he brought them out from their distress; he made the storm be still, and the waves of the sea were hushed. Then they were glad because they had quiet, and God brought them to their "desired haven." (Ps 107:26–30)

The sea had a further association: not only was it a powerful force that threatened human life, but sometimes it was explicitly associated with evil. We see this especially in the book of Daniel. In Daniel's vision in chapter seven, "four great beasts came up out of the sea." The monstrous beasts represent four foreign empires that ruled the Jewish people from the exile onward.

Language from Daniel 7 is used by the author of Revelation in the New Testament. In Revelation 13, a beast with ten horns and seven heads rises "out of the sea," rules the world, and makes war on the saints. In its first-century setting, this beast from "the sea" is clearly the Roman Empire.

The Story

The metaphorical meanings of "the sea" are all part of the context for understanding Mark 4:35–41.

> [35] On that day, when evening had come, he said to them, "Let us go across to the other side." [36] And leaving the crowd behind, they took him with them in the boat, just as he was. Other boats were with him. [37] A great windstorm arose, and the waves beat into the boat, so that the boat was already being swamped. [38] But he was in the stern, asleep on the cushion; and they woke him up and said to him, "Teacher, do you not care that we are perishing?" [39] He woke up and rebuked the wind, and said to the sea, "Peace! Be still!" Then the wind ceased, and there was a dead calm. [40] He said to them, "Why are you afraid? Have you still no faith?" [41] And they were filled with great awe and said to one another, "Who then is this, that even the wind and the sea obey him?"

The story is filled with fear. It is night, dark. The disciples are on the sea and a storm comes up. Waves crash into their boat and threaten to swamp it. Fearing they are in mortal danger, they cry out to Jesus who is asleep in the stern: "Do you not care that we are perishing?"

Awakened, Jesus rebuked the wind and silenced the sea. Then he addressed the disciples: "Why are you afraid? Have you still no faith?" Fear and lack of faith go together; so also faith and courage go together.

Interestingly and importantly, the language of rebuking and silencing the sea is the same language used in Mark 1:25 as Jesus rebuked and silenced a demon. The stilling of the sea is linguistically connected to the overcoming of the demonic.

The Exorcism of Legion: 5:1–20

That this story of Jesus casting out a legion of demons and sending them into the sea immediately follows Jesus' stilling the sea is thus not coincidental or accidental. Though it begins a new chapter, it is not a separate topic but organically related to the preceding story.

In verse one, Jesus and his disciples "came to the other side of the lake, to the country of the Gerasenes." Then, in the longest and most fully developed exorcism story in the gospels, we are told:

[2] And when he had stepped out of the boat, immediately a man out of the tombs with an unclean spirit met him. [3] He lived among the tombs; and no one could restrain him any more, even with a chain;

[4] for he had often been restrained with shackles and chains, but the chains he wrenched apart, and the shackles he broke in pieces; and no one had the strength to subdue him. [5] Night and day among the tombs and on the mountains he was always howling and bruising himself with stones. [6] When he saw Jesus from a distance, he ran and bowed down before him; [7] and he shouted at the top of his voice, "What have you to do with me, Jesus, Son of the Most High God? I adjure you by God, do not torment me." [8] For he had said to him, "Come out of the man, you unclean spirit!" [9] Then Jesus asked him, "What is your name?" He replied, "My name is Legion; for we are many." [10] He begged him earnestly not to send them out of the country. [11] Now there on the hillside a great herd of swine was feeding; [12] and the unclean spirits begged him, "Send us into

the swine; let us enter them." [13] So he gave them permission. And the unclean spirits came out and entered the swine; and the herd, numbering about two thousand, rushed down the steep bank into the sea, and were drowned in the sea. [14] The swineherds ran off and told it in the city and in the country. Then people came to see what it was that had happened. [15] They came to Jesus and saw the demoniac sitting there, clothed and in his right mind, the very man who had had the legion; and they were afraid. [16] Those who had seen what had happened to the demoniac and to the swine reported it. [17] Then they began to beg Jesus to leave their neighborhood. [18] As he was getting into the boat, the man who had been possessed by demons begged him that he might be with him. [19] But Jesus refused, and said to him, "Go home to your friends, and tell them how much the Lord has done for you, and what mercy he has shown you" [20] And he went away and began to proclaim in the Decapolis how much Jesus had done for him; and everyone was amazed.

Some features are common to stories of possession and exorcism. The demoniac has more-than-human strength: he breaks the chains with which he is shackled and no one can subdue him. He has more-than-human knowledge: he knows that Jesus is "Son of the Most High God," even though no human in Mark's gospel has yet addressed Jesus that way.

The more specific details in the story highlight the theme of purity and impurity, a contrast also expressed as clean and unclean. Within Jewish law and practice, these opposites applied to persons, places, and things.

Importantly, impurity was not the same as sin. Some activities that are ordinary, even unavoidable, created impurity without being sinful or wrong. For example, sexual intercourse and menstruation created a temporary condition of impurity, but were not sinful. So also did touching a corpse—and yet doing so was sometimes necessary: burying one's father was a sacred obligation. But though impurity was not sinful, it was contagious: it defiled, made one unclean. It had power.

Mark has already introduced this theme in his first three chapters. There Jesus touches an unclean leper (1:40–45), eats with unclean people (2:15–17), and is accused of being possessed by an unclean spirit (3:22–30).

Now, in this text, Mark returns to the theme. Its details paint a picture of pervasive impurity.

- *Geography.* Jesus and his disciples have crossed the sea from Jewish territory to Gentile territory. Gentile territory was impure compared to the greater purity of "the holy land."
- *Possession.* The demoniac is possessed by "an unclean spirit."
- *Proximity to corpses.* He lives among tombs, in a cemetery defiled by the presence of corpses. According to the custom of the time, stepping on a grave made one impure.
- *Name.* The name of the demoniac is "Legion." A legion was a large Roman military unit (like the modern military term "division"), and thus his name refers to the pagan and impure imperial power that controlled that part of the world. He and the land itself are possessed by "Legion."
- *Animals.* There are pigs—lots of them—in the area. Pigs are unclean animals.

> **Legion:** a Roman military unit, commonly made up of 6,000 troops

In this scene of overwhelming impurity, Jesus exorcises Legion and sends the legion of unclean spirits into a herd of two thousand swine who rush into the sea and drown. With them gone, the man is restored to his right mind and returned to community.

As a metaphorical narrative, a parabolic narrative, the central meaning of the story is clear: Jesus overcomes impurity. Though impurity is contagious, the power of the Spirit in Jesus is stronger than impurity. This theme continues through the rest of Mark 5.

There may be another meaning as well, signaled by the name "Legion." As already noted, this is an unmistakable allusion to the Roman Empire and its possession of the Jewish homeland. Are we to think that the story of Jesus as a whole is about expelling Roman imperial domination—not through the violence of armed revolt, but through proclamation of the kingdom of God as the alternative to the kingdoms and empires of this world? Is this story about both personal and political possession, and the exorcism of "Legion" as the path of both personal and political liberation?

To conclude our exploration of this text, we return for a moment to the question of factual interpretation versus parabolic interpretation.

If we were to read this story factually, a number of difficult questions arise. Is there such a thing as a legion of demons? Can they be sent into a herd of pigs? And though the demoniac benefits from the exorcism, what about the swineherds and the owner(s) of the pigs, who suffered a considerable financial loss? But these are idle questions, and they distract from the meaning of the story. Indeed, these questions disappear when we read the story as a parable about Jesus.

Healings of Two Women

The rest of Mark 5 reports the healings of two women. One is the twelve-year-old daughter of a synagogue leader named Jairus. The other is an adult woman with a flow of blood that has continued for twelve years. Mark weaves these stories together by embedding one within the other. He begins the story of Jairus' daughter in 5:21–24, then tells the story of the woman with a flow in verses 25–34, and then resumes the story of Jairus' daughter in verses 35–43. This is sometimes called a "sandwich" technique: two slices of bread surround what is in between.

Mark does this quite often. Look back to Mark 3, where he sandwiches the story of scribes from Jerusalem who accuse Jesus of being possessed by "the ruler of the demons" (3:22) in between material about his family (3:21 and 3:31–35). Look forward to Mark 11, where Mark surrounds the story of Jesus' disrupting the moneychangers in the temple (11:15–19) with the cursing of the fig tree (11:12–14, 11:20–25). The effect of this technique: readers are encouraged to interpret the stories that make up the sandwich together.

We return to Mark 5 and begin with the story in the middle of his sandwich: the woman with a constant flow of blood (5:25–34). The severity of her condition is underlined. She has been hemorrhaging for twelve years, she has tried many doctors but has only gotten worse, and she is impoverished: "she had spent all that she had" (verses 25–26). Then, hearing that Jesus is passing by, she comes up behind him in desperation and touches his cloak. Immediately she is healed. The story ends with Jesus' words to her: "Daughter, your faith has made you well; go in peace."

The story has a number of meanings:

- *Purity and impurity.* It continues the theme of purity and impurity that we saw in the story of Legion. The woman's constant flow of blood—like menstruation—made her impure, and she had endured this malady for twelve years. Like the demoniac living among tombs, her condition isolated her.

  Moreover, recall that according to the conventions of the time, impurity was contagious: Jesus should have been made impure by the woman touching his cloak. But the reverse happens: her impurity is overcome through contact with Jesus. Once again, Jesus banishes impurity and rescues the impure.

- *The importance of stories of women in the gospels.* Luke emphasizes this most, but Mark focuses on women too. Back in his first chapter, he reports that Jesus healed Peter's mother-in-law. Now Jesus heals this woman (and soon the daughter of Jairus). In Mark 7, he will heal the daughter of a Gentile woman. In the last week of his life, he will be anointed for burial by a woman (14:3). Finally, women (not the male disciples—they all flee) witness Jesus' crucifixion, and women are the first to be told of his resurrection.

- *The importance of faith.* A third meaning of this story is embedded in these words of Jesus to the woman: "Daughter, your faith has made you well." And what was her faith? The conviction that Jesus could heal her and restore her to community. This is not faith as belief in a set of doctrines. This is faith as confidence in Jesus. The woman's faith contrasts with the fear of the disciples on a stormy sea: "Why are you afraid?" Jesus demands of them. "Have you still no faith?" (4:40).

The importance of women in early Christianity is also found in Paul's seven genuine letters. In later letters attributed to Paul, women are subordinated to men. But in the letters that all scholars agree go back to Paul, women are patrons of the Jesus movement (Phoebe in Romans 16:1), prophets (1 Corinthians 11:1–10), and even apostles (Junia in Romans 16:7).

We turn now to the outer layers of Mark's sandwich, his framing the story of the woman with a flow of blood for twelve years with the story of the twelve-year-old daughter of Jairus. The fact that the number twelve appears in both stories underlines their connection.

Jairus is "one of the leaders of the synagogue" (5:22). In first-century Jewish Galilee, a synagogue was an assembly, a gathering, and not necessarily a building. Moreover, to be a leader of a synagogue need not mean that Jairus was a particularly important person or a member of "the elite." Most likely, he was one of the leaders of a village synagogue and no doubt a devout Jew.

Jairus tells Jesus that his daughter is near death and begs Jesus to come with him so that he can lay hands on her "so that she may be made well and live" (5:23). Jesus goes with him. Then, after Mark has told the story of the woman with a flow of blood, messengers report to Jairus that his daughter has died (5:35). Jesus tells Jairus, "Do not fear; only believe" (5:36). Fear and its opposite—faith—are the same theme we have heard in the stories of the stilling of the storm and the healing of the woman with a flow of blood.

They arrive at Jairus' home, where mourners are already grieving his daughter's death, "weeping and wailing loudly." But Jesus says, "Why do you make a commotion and weep? The child is not dead, but sleeping." The crowd laughs at him: of course the girl is dead. But Jesus takes her by the hand and says, "Little girl, get up!" And immediately she does (5:41).

The language of "not dead, but sleeping" is ambiguous. Was the child not really dead, but only in a coma, which Jesus recognized? Or was she really dead, but Jesus raised her, so that this was his first raising of somebody from the dead? To ask these questions is perhaps to miss the meaning of the story.

Rather, this story's location in Mark points to its meanings. It is the last in the series of miracle stories that began with the stilling of the storm near the end of Mark 4. This suggests that its meanings are related to the central themes of that series. One of those themes, as we have seen, is Jesus and the overcoming of impurity.

That impurity is a theme of this story is confirmed by two details. Mark uses it to "sandwich" the story of the woman with a flow, where impurity is the central issue. The parts of Mark's sandwiches interpret each other. Moreover, Jairus' daughter is said to be dead, and according to the conventions of the time, touching a corpse made you impure. But Jesus touches her. She is restored to life—just as the demoniac was restored to life in community and the woman with a flow to a life beyond her isolation.

A second theme of this series of miracle stories is the power of Jesus over the forces that stand opposed to God. He has power over the sea and evil spirits; he rebukes and silences both. He has power over Legion. He has power over impurity. He has power over death. Or was she only sleeping? He has power to awaken people to new life. As chapter five ends, Mark has announced all the central themes of his gospel. In our next chapter, we will see these themes again, together with the story of the execution of John the Baptizer, thereby once again anticipating the conflict that will end Jesus' life.

CHAPTER THREE

Rejection, Miracles, and Conflict: Mark 6:1–8:21

As chapter 6 of Mark begins—and all the way through 8:21—we are still in Galilee. Soon Jesus will begin his final journey to Jerusalem. But not yet. We begin with an overview of the topics we'll find in Mark 6:

- Jesus is rejected in his home village of Nazareth (6:1–6)
- Jesus sends the twelve disciples, two by two, on a mission of exorcism (6:7–13)
- John the Baptizer is executed by Herod Antipas (6:14–29)
- Jesus feeds five thousand people with a few loaves and fish (6:30–44)
- Jesus performs his second sea miracle, as the disciples, again caught in a storm on the sea, witness Jesus coming to them walking on the water (6:45–52)
- A summary report of many healings (6:53–56)

In much of Mark 7, the main theme is purity and impurity, as it was in Mark 5. And, as in Mark 2–3, chapter 7 contains stories of conflict with the Pharisees:

■ Pharisees accuse Jesus' disciples of eating with "defiled" hands—that is, with unclean and impure hands (7:1–8)

■ Jesus criticizes Pharisees for their preoccupation with purity while at the same time finding ways to avoid observing more important obligations (7:9–13)

■ Jesus negates the common understanding of purity (7:14–15), then follows with an explanation to the disciples (7:17–23)

Mark 7 concludes with two healing stories:

■ A Gentile woman begs Jesus to cast an evil spirit out of her daughter; he at first refuses, and then changes his mind (7:24–30)

■ Jesus heals a deaf man with a speech impediment (7:31–37)

To conclude our overview, the portion of Mark 8 we are exploring in this chapter includes:

■ A second feeding miracle: in this one, Jesus feeds four thousand people with a few loaves and fish (8:1–10)

■ Pharisees test Jesus by asking for "a sign from heaven." Jesus refuses (8:11–13)

■ Jesus warns the disciples about the "yeast," or leaven, of the Pharisees and Herod (8:14–21). The disciples misunderstand and Jesus berates them for not "getting it." His indictment of the disciples is harsh: "Are your hearts hardened? Do you have eyes and fail to see? Do you have ears, and fail to hear? . . . Do you not yet understand?" (8:17–18, 21)

Much of the material in these chapters is foreboding. Though there are healings and nature miracles, there are also themes of rejection, conflict, and misunderstanding, picking up once again on the conflict stories found in Mark 2–3.

Rejection at Nazareth: Mark 6:1–6

Mark 6 begins with Jesus leaving Jairus' village: "He left that place and came to his hometown, and his disciples followed him." Then, "On the sabbath he began to teach in the synagogue. . . ."

The "hometown" of Jesus was Nazareth. The gospels differ on how Jesus happened to live in Nazareth. According to Luke, Nazareth was the home of Mary and Joseph before Jesus was born, and he was born in Bethlehem only because of the taxation census ordered by Caesar Augustus. But according to Matthew, the home of Mary and Joseph when Jesus was born was Bethlehem, and the family moved to Nazareth after taking refuge in Egypt because of the vicious reputation of Herod the Great's son Archelaus, ruler of the area that included Bethlehem. But regardless of how Jesus got to Nazareth, all the gospels agree that he was from Nazareth. He is "Jesus of Nazareth," not "Jesus of Bethlehem." Indeed, many scholars think he may have been born in Nazareth. In any case, he grew up there.

Archeology indicates that Nazareth was small—a village of perhaps two hundred to four hundred people. It was about five miles from the largest city in Galilee, Sepphoris, which had been conquered and at least partially destroyed by Roman legions in the year 4 B.C.E. as they suppressed the revolt that broke out after Herod the Great's death. Rebuilt soon afterward, Sepphoris was the capital of Herod Antipas' kingdom until he moved his capital to Tiberias on the Sea of Galilee around the year 20 C.E., when Jesus was in his twenties.

As in peasant villages generally, the inhabitants of Nazareth were mostly agricultural workers with some other manual laborers and "artisans," a skilled working class. If the tradition that Jesus and his father Joseph were carpenters is correct (the Greek word could also mean "stonecutter"), they were from that class. To be a carpenter (or stonecutter) does not mean that they were "middle class" compared to agricultural workers. Most often, artisans came from peasant families who had lost their land.

Artisan: a skilled manual laborer: carpenter, stonecutter, potter, and so forth

Nazareth was so small that it may not have had any public buildings. The reference to Jesus teaching "in the synagogue" may simply mean that he spoke in the village assembly on the sabbath, not necessarily in a building.

According to Mark 6:2, his hometown's initial perception of Jesus was positive: "Many who heard him were astounded. They said,

'Where did this man get all this? What is this wisdom that has been given to him? What deeds of power are being done by his hands!'"

Then their perception changes and becomes negative:

> ³ Is not this the carpenter, the son of Mary and brother of James and Joses and Judas and Simon, and are not his sisters here with us?" And they took offense at him. ⁴ Then Jesus said to them, "Prophets are not without honor, except in their hometown, and among their own kin, and in their own house." ⁵ And he could do no deed of power there, except that he laid his hands on a few sick people and cured them. ⁶ And he was amazed at their unbelief.

The passage includes a number of surprises. After the initial positive impression of Jesus, "they took offense at him," but we are not told why. Luke in his longer account of Jesus in Nazareth (Luke 4:16–30) reports a similar shift from a positive to a negative perception, again without explaining the reason.

A second surprise: Jesus is called "the son of Mary," not the son of Joseph. This is unusual in the ancient world—a man was commonly known as son of his father, not son of his mother. The usual explanation is that Joseph must have died when Jesus was quite young, and so he was known as "son of Mary." Another surprise: Jesus had brothers and sisters. Though Protestants have long thought so, Catholics have commonly believed that Jesus was an only child because of the perpetual virginity of Mary.

And yet another surprise: Mark says that Jesus "*could* do no deed of power there." As Matthew copies this story from Mark, he says that Jesus "*did* not do many deeds of power there, because of their unbelief" (Matt. 13:58). Matthew's implication is clear: Jesus *could have, but didn't*. Matthew seeks to avoid the impression that Jesus' power was limited in any way.

To their negative perception, Jesus responds: "Prophets are not without honor, except in their hometown, and among their own kin, and in their own house." These words identify Jesus with the prophets of ancient Israel, the first time this has happened in Mark; and it affirms that prophets are often rejected. So it is with Jesus: he is rejected by his own, as he was by Pharisees and scribes in Mark 2–3, by his family in 3:21, and as he will be in the concluding chapters of Mark's gospel.

The Execution of the Baptizer: Mark 6:14–29

The theme of conflict and rejection continues in the story of the execution of John the Baptizer. It is a tawdry tale: a royal divorce involving a king marrying his brother's wife, a queen's wrath, a king's birthday banquet, a dancing girl, a rash royal promise—and all of this climaxing with the head of John the Baptizer delivered to the banquet on a platter.

As the story begins, John has already been executed. We are told that "King Herod" (as Mark calls Herod Antipas) has heard of Jesus and wonders if he might be John the Baptizer raised from the dead: "John, whom I beheaded, has been raised," he speculates (6:16). Does Mark mean that Herod believed that Jesus was literally John the Baptizer raised from the dead? Hard to know. But at the very least, it means that Herod wondered if Jesus was going to be John "all over again." Would the same spirit that had been in John, he wondered, be in Jesus too?

As Herod ponders, Mark gives us a flashback to John's execution. Though the details of the story are not crucially important, they are interesting:

- Herod Antipas marries his brother Philip's wife, Herodias. Like Herod Antipas, Philip was one of Herod the Great's sons who was given part of Herod's kingdom when he died. Herodias had been Philip's wife and queen—but now Herod Antipas had wooed her away.
- John was in prison, arrested by Herod Antipas because he had become a critic of his marriage. Herodias wanted John killed. But Herod was reluctant.
- At Herod's birthday banquet, Herodias' daughter dances for the crowd of courtiers, officers, and the leaders of Galilee. Later tradition gives her the name "Salome," though she is unnamed in the gospels.
- Salome so pleases Herod and his guests that the king offers to give her anything she wants, "even half of my kingdom." She confers with her mother Herodias, Herod's wife and queen, who tells her to ask for John the Baptizer's head. The deed is done.

■ John's disciples hear about his death, claim his body, and place it in a tomb.

Within Mark's gospel, this story foreshadows the execution of Jesus. Of course, the details are different. But John had been the mentor of Jesus, and now he has been executed by the ruler of his world. And, according to Mark 1:14, Jesus began his public activity only after John had been arrested—he saw himself in some sense as continuing what John had begun. John's execution points to how dangerous the task and message were—if Herod has done this to John, can Jesus expect any better treatment from the powers that ruled his world?

The Feeding of the Five Thousand: Mark 6:30–44

This is the second "nature miracle" in Mark; the stilling of the storm in 4:35–41 was the first. It is also the first of two "bread miracles" in Mark, in which Jesus feeds a crowd of thousands with a few loaves and fish. The second is later in this section of Mark, 8:1–10.

Because of the spectacular features of this story—Jesus feeds five thousand people with five loaves and two fish, with twelve baskets full of leftovers—we begin with a reminder. Recall our conversation in the last chapter about treating the nature miracles as parables about Jesus—as parabolic stories, their point lies in their meanings. So, as you read this story, believe whatever you want about whether the feeding of five thousand happened exactly this way—and then, let's talk about its meanings.

At the beginning of the story, the twelve (here called "the apostles") return from their mission of casting out evil spirits in Mark 6:7–13:

> [30] The apostles gathered around Jesus, and told him all that they had done and taught. [31] He said to them, "Come away to a deserted place all by yourselves and rest a while." For many were coming and going, and they had no leisure even to eat. [32] And they went away in the boat to a deserted place by themselves. [33] Now many saw them going and recognized them, and they hurried there on foot from all the towns and arrived ahead of them.
>
> [34] As he went ashore, he saw a great crowd; and he had compassion for them, because they were like sheep without a shepherd; and he

began to teach them many things. [35] When it grew late, his disciples came to him and said, "This is a deserted place, and the hour is now very late; [36] send them away so that they may go into the surrounding country and villages and buy something for themselves to eat."

[37] But he answered them, "You give them something to eat." They said to him, "Are we to go and buy two hundred denarii worth of bread, and give it to them to eat?" [38] And he said to them, "How many loaves have you? Go and see." When they had found out, they said, "Five, and two fish." [39] Then he ordered them to get all the people to sit down in groups on the green grass. [40] So they sat down in groups of hundreds and of fifties. [41] Taking the five loaves and the two fish, he looked up to heaven, and blessed and broke the loaves, and gave them to his disciples to set before the people; and he divided the two fish among them all. [42] And all ate and were filled; [43] and they took up twelve baskets full of broken pieces and of the fish. [44] Those who had eaten the loaves numbered five thousand men.

More-Than-Literal Meanings

This story has multiple themes and meanings.

- *Jesus provides spiritual food.* Mark twice mentions that the setting is "a deserted place" (verses 32, 35), where Jesus feeds a multitude. The theme of bread in the wilderness goes back to the story of Moses and the exodus from Egypt. In ancient Israel's primal narrative, we are told that God fed the ancestors of Israel with manna in the wilderness. Manna is a mysterious substance in the exodus story: it falls from the sky each morning, and provides all the nourishment the wanderers needed to live.

  So the feeding story in Mark associates Jesus with Moses and the exodus. Jesus, the story implies, is like a new Moses who feeds the people of God in the wilderness even as he also challenges the Pharaoh who ruled his world by proclaiming the kingdom of God. Matthew develops the theme of Jesus as a new Moses and the gospel as a new exodus most fully, but that theme is also present here in Mark.

- In the gospel of John, the allusion to bread/manna in the wilderness becomes explicit. His version of this story is much longer, filling most of his sixth chapter, and the phrase "manna in the wilderness" is used both by the crowd and Jesus (John 6:31–32, 49). John, unlike Mark, reports that Jesus said about himself, "I am the bread of life" (6:35, 48), "the bread that came down from heaven" (6:41, 50, 58). So in John, Jesus himself is the bread. Indeed, the Jesus of John even speaks of the necessity of eating his flesh and drinking his blood (6:51–57). For John, this story of wilderness feeding is about Jesus himself as spiritual food and drink.

- *Jesus provides physical food.* Though Mark's story echoes the exodus theme of manna in the wilderness, it is not yet about Jesus as spiritual food. It is—and this is a second theme— about *feeding* people. Bread—real bread as food, the material basis of life—mattered to Jesus.

Enough bread, enough food, was the central survival issue in the exploited and impoverished peasant class to whom Jesus mostly spoke. Bread—real bread—is central to the coming of the kingdom of God. In the Lord's Prayer, in all its three ancient versions (Matthew 6, Luke 11, and Diadache 8:2, an early Christian document not included in the New Testament),

Diadache: the word means "teaching" and also refers to an early Christian document written around the year 100

"Give us our daily bread" immediately follows the petition for the coming of God's kingdom. God's kingdom means bread for the world.

In this context, the conversation between Jesus and his disciples is important: they think it's impossible to feed the multitude, and ask Jesus to send the people away because there's nothing to eat. Jesus responds, "You give them something to eat." And they object—it isn't possible, they insist, for even two hundred *denarii* wouldn't buy enough food (one *denarius* was the average daily wage). Jesus ignores their objections and asks them how many loaves they had. The answer: "Five, and two fish." The miracle: all five thousand are fed, and the leftovers exceed what they began with. The point: when bread—food— passes through the hands of Jesus, there is enough for everybody. This is a story about bread for the world.

- *The eucharist is a real meal.* There is a third meaning as well. The language of taking, blessing, breaking, and distributing resonates with early Christian observance of the Lord's Supper, variously named by Christians as the mass, Eucharist, or communion. Importantly, the Lord's Supper in early Christianity was a real meal, not simply a morsel of wafer and a sip of wine. The Lord's Supper as a real meal points once again to the importance of food for Jesus and early Christianity.

Of course, according to the gospels, Jesus also said, "One does not live by bread alone" (Matt 4:4, Luke 4:4). True. Yet bread—real bread, real food—mattered to Jesus and his audience. The kingdom of God as bread for the world is not just about spiritual food, but real food. In the gospels, it is always about both.

The Second Sea Miracle: Mark 6:45–52

[45] Immediately he made his disciples get into the boat and go on ahead to the other side, to Bethsaida, while he dismissed the crowd.

[46] After saying farewell to them, he went up on the mountain to pray.

[47] When evening came, the boat was out on the sea, and he was alone on the land. [48] When he saw that they were straining at the oars against an adverse wind, he came towards them early in the morning, walking on the sea. He intended to pass them by. [49] But when they saw him walking on the sea, they thought it was a ghost and cried out;

[50] for they all saw him and were terrified. But immediately he spoke to them and said, "Take heart, it is I; do not be afraid." [51] Then he got into the boat with them and the wind ceased. And they were utterly astounded, [52] for they did not understand about the loaves, but their hearts were hardened.

This story is similar to the story of Jesus stilling a storm in Mark 4:35–41, with one significant difference. In the earlier story, Jesus was with the disciples in the boat, but asleep. In this one, the disciples are on their own. Alone, they struggle vainly against an adverse wind, all night long, until "early in the morning." Then Jesus comes to them walking on the water, gets into the boat and the wind ceases. The disciples are saved.

All the comments in Chapter 2 about the ominous significance of the sea in Jewish tradition are relevant to this story as well. Once again, the sea threatens to overwhelm the disciples. Once again they hear a message about courage and fear: Jesus' first words to them are, "Take heart, it is I; do not be afraid."

This meaning is amplified by an episode that Matthew adds as he copies Mark's story into his own gospel. In Matthew 14:28–31, Peter also walks on the water. After Jesus says, "Do not be afraid," Matthew tells us:

> [28] Peter answered him, "Lord, if it is you, command me to come to you on the water." [29] He [Jesus] said, "Come." So Peter got out of the boat, started walking on the water, and came toward Jesus.
>
> [30] But when he noticed the strong wind, he became frightened, and beginning to sink, he cried out, "Lord, save me!" [31] Jesus immediately reached out his hand and caught him, saying, "You of little faith, why did you doubt?"

For a while, Peter walks on water, but as he "became frightened," he began to sink. After rescuing him, Jesus addressed him as "you of little faith." The connection is clear: fear, lack of courage, and "little faith" go together. With little faith, you become frightened and sink.

What does this episode mean? Consider two options. If we hear the story factually, it means that Peter was literally able to walk on water until he became afraid. If that's the right way of hearing the story, then what would it mean for us? Is it simply a report of a spectacular and unrepeatable event? A piece of information about the past? One of those miraculous things that happened in biblical times? And if it is a factual report, does it mean that we could walk on water if we have sufficient faith and don't become afraid? Or was that feat possible only then, and only for Peter?

The second option is to hear the passage metaphorically as a parabolic story. Setting aside the question of factuality, its meaning is clear—we can express it in many ways:

- Faith and fear are opposites.
- Faith and courage go together.
- Faith enables us to overcome the stormy sea.
- Without faith, we sink.
- Faith is trusting in the buoyancy of God.

Matthew's addition of the story of Peter walking on the water until he became frightened insightfully amplifies Mark's meaning.

A further meaning of this passage is suggested by the difference between this story and the first sea miracle. In the early centuries of Christianity, a boat or a ship was sometimes used as a symbol of the church—the Christian community. Remember that Jesus is not in the boat as this story begins. So Mark's story of the disciples "straining at the oars against an adverse wind" (6:48) suggests what happens when Jesus isn't there—they were completely stalled and in mortal danger. But with Jesus in the boat, "the wind ceased" (6:51) and they were able to make it across the sea to safe haven. The meaning and moral of the story: Keep Jesus in the boat—don't set out without him. You won't make it.

Conflict about Purity: Mark 7:1–23

Just as the first sea miracle in 4:35–41 was followed by a sequence of stories about the contrast between purity and impurity in Mark 5, so the second sea miracle is also followed by an extended section of confrontations about the meaning of purity. At the beginning of Mark 7, "Pharisees and some of the scribes who had come from Jerusalem" criticize Jesus' disciples for "eating with defiled hands, that is, without washing them" (7:1–4). The issue was not hygiene, but purity. The purity laws of the Pharisees included the ritual washing of hands before eating, and they wonder why Jesus and his disciples do "not live according to the tradition of the elders, but eat with defiled hands?" (7:5).

Jesus responds by quoting Isaiah 29:13:

> [6] He said to them, "Isaiah prophesied rightly about you hypocrites, as it is written, 'This people honors me with their lips, but their hearts are far from me; [7] in vain do they worship me, teaching human precepts as doctrines.' [8] You abandon the commandment of God and hold to human tradition."

Jesus reviles his critics as "hypocrites"—a common early-Christian invective directed at Pharisees and scribes, often to extremes, as in Matthew 23. In modern English, the word commonly refers to people who pretend a righteousness that is not real, who don't practice what they preach—a "phony." As a blanket indictment of Pharisees, it is unfair. Most Pharisees practiced what they preached. Some, perhaps many, were deeply devout. Some became martyrs because of their loyalty to the God of Israel. Some were Jewish saints. But in this passage, Jesus calls some of them "you hypocrites." As used here, the text from Isaiah makes a threefold indictment against Jesus' critics:

- They honor God with their lips, but their hearts are far from God.
- Their worship is vanity because they teach "human precepts as doctrines."
- They "abandon the commandment of God" by holding to "human tradition."

This seems like a strong response to a conflict about washing hands. But the issue is larger: the purity laws of the scribes and Pharisees are named as "human precepts" and "human tradition" that get in the way of observing "the commandment of God."

Mark's use of the singular "*the commandment* of God" seems deliberate, for he repeats the phrase in the next verse as the conflict escalates. Citing a practice known as "Corban," Jesus accuses his critics of "rejecting the commandment of God" in order to keep their tradition (7:8). This allowed persons to dedicate their wealth as an offering to God in order to avoid financially supporting their parents in their old age—one of the central meanings of the commandment, "Honor your father and your mother." But the Pharisees have found a way around this sacred obligation with their teachings. "And you do many things like this," Jesus declares as the text concludes (7:10–13).

Corban: dedicated to God

The issue broadens even further in the next two verses:

> [14] Then he called the crowd again and said to them, "Listen to me, all of you, and understand: [15] there is nothing outside a person that by going in can defile, but the things that come out are what defile."

More than one scholar has called verse 15 one of the most radical sayings in the teaching of Jesus. The reason: it radically re-defines purity. Purity is not about the observance of laws that separate a person from what is impure and unclean. Rather, Jesus insists, "There is nothing outside a person that by going in can defile." Instead, it is "the things that come out [of a person]" that defile. What matters is "the inside," or "the heart," as Mark calls it a few verses later. That's what Jesus means when he says in Matthew 5:8: "Blessed are the pure in heart."

In the historical context of Mark and Jesus, this is revolutionary. Purity laws were part of the conventions of the time, and they were intensified by religious groups such as the Pharisees and Essenes, a Jewish religious group dedicated to simple living, voluntary poverty, and abstinence from worldly pleasures. The society of Jesus' time was to a considerable extent shaped by purity laws. This redefinition subverted those laws and the sharp social boundaries created by their observance.

> **Essenes:** Jewish group who left society in order to live in communities dedicated to holiness

Mark emphasizes this subversive redefinition of purity by having Jesus explain and expand the saying to the disciples:

> [18] "Do you not see that whatever goes into a person from outside cannot defile, [19] since it enters, not **the heart** but the stomach, and goes out into the sewer?" (Thus he declared all foods clean.)
>
> [20] And he said, "It is what comes out of a person that defiles.
>
> [21] For it is **from within, from the human heart,** that evil intentions come."

Within the parentheses in this passage, Mark applies the meaning of Jesus' declaration about purity to clean (*kosher*) and unclean food, but this remark about food probably does not originate in the time of Jesus. There is no evidence or reason to think that Jesus abolished the notion of kosher; if he had, then the disputes about kosher food in early Christianity become inexplicable. Rather, the passage has a broader meaning than clean and unclean food: purity is about the "within," "the heart," the inside—that's what matters.

The Exorcism of a Gentile Woman's Daughter: 7:24–30

The long section on purity is followed by another exorcism story, set outside the traditional boundaries of the Jewish homeland, to the north of Galilee, in the region of Tyre near the Mediterranean Sea in present-day Lebanon. Mark does not tell us why Jesus went there, though his comment that Jesus "did not want anyone to know he was there" may suggest that he was seeking either refuge or rest.

²⁴ From there he set out and went away to the region of Tyre. He entered a house and did not want anyone to know he was there. Yet he could not escape notice, ²⁵ but a woman whose little daughter had an unclean spirit immediately heard about him, and she came and bowed down at his feet. ²⁶ Now the woman was a Gentile, of Syrophoenician origin. She begged him to cast the demon out of her daughter. ²⁷ He said to her, "Let the children be fed first, for it is not fair to take the children's food and throw it to the dogs." ²⁸ But she answered him, "Sir, even the dogs under the table eat the children's crumbs." ²⁹ Then he said to her, "For saying that, you may go; the demon has left your daughter." ³⁰ So she went home, found the child lying on the bed, and the demon gone.

The story has a number of striking features:

- The woman who asks Jesus to exorcise her daughter is a Gentile. This is only the second story in Mark involving a Gentile (the other: 5:1–20).
- Jesus initially rebuffs her: "Let the children be fed first, for it is not fair to take the children's food and throw it to the dogs." In context, the meaning is clear: "the children" are the Jewish people, and it was to his own people that Jesus saw his primary mission. Indeed, in Matthew, he tells his followers "Go nowhere among the Gentiles . . . but go rather to the lost sheep of the house of Israel" (Matt 10:5–6) and affirms about himself, "I was sent only to the lost sheep of the house of Israel" (Matt 15:24). And just as "the children" are Jews, so Gentiles are "dogs"—and dogs were not well-regarded in Jesus' world.
- The woman, undeterred, retorts: "Sir, even the dogs under the table eat the children's crumbs."
- Jesus changes his mind and tells her that her daughter has been healed. Feminist scholars have pointed out that this is the only story in the gospels where Jesus changes his mind— and it was a Gentile woman who led him to do so.

Healing, Feeding, Conflict: Mark 7:31–8:21

We turn now to a summary of the rest of this section that began with 6:1. The stories in 7:31–8:21 are about healing, feeding, conflict, and misunderstanding.

■ *Healing.* In 7:31–37, Jesus heals a person who is both deaf and mute. Using physical means and looking up to heaven, Jesus "put his fingers into his ears, and he spat and touched his tongue." The man is healed. The story concludes with the exclamation: "He even makes the deaf to hear and the mute to speak."

■ *Feeding.* Mark narrates a second feeding miracle (8:1–10). Just as the first and second sea miracles are similar, with a few differences in the details, so also here. Once again a great multitude is without food in the desert. Once again, the disciples cannot imagine how they can be fed: "How can one feed these people with bread here in the desert?" Once again, a few loaves and fish are available. Once again, Jesus takes the loaves, gives thanks, breaks them, and gives them to the disciples to distribute. The result: "They [the multitude] ate and were filled."

The differences are largely in Mark's use of numbers in this story. Verse 2 says that the crowd had nothing to eat "for three days." (Note that "three days" is often a symbolic number in the Bible, though its symbolic meaning here is unclear.) In the first story, the multitude numbered five thousand—here, four thousand. In the first story, five loaves were involved—here, seven. In the first story, there were twelve baskets full of leftovers—here, seven. Scholars have puzzled about the possible meanings of these numbers without reaching any widely accepted explanations. They remain mysterious.

■ *Conflict.* Immediately after the feeding story, Pharisees reappear in Mark's narrative (8:11–12). They argue with Jesus, asking him for "a sign from heaven, to test him." Jesus refuses, asking, "Why does this generation ask for a sign? Truly I tell you, no sign will be given to this generation."

What does this exchange mean? What were the Pharisees asking for? A "miracle" from Jesus in order to establish his credentials and prove himself? But what about all the previous miracles reported in Mark, some of which were public? Shouldn't they be enough? Are the Pharisees asking for a miracle done in front of their eyes, a private performance for their benefit? Hard to know.

What is clear is Jesus' refusal. But why? Because he wouldn't do a miracle to prove something, but only to help somebody? Or because he couldn't do a spectacular deed in the presence of unbelief, as occurred in Nazareth? Or something more?

The refusal to provide "a sign" means at least this: if people don't "get it" from the message and presence of Jesus, then they won't "get it" from a miracle. They will find a way to discount it—as they did by attributing Jesus' exorcisms to an evil power in 3:22.

Whatever the meaning of the Pharisees' request and Jesus' refusal, the episode re-introduces the theme of conflict. In the final story of this section, the conflict is augmented by the misunderstanding of the disciples.

■ *Misunderstanding.* Mark 8:13–21 begins with Jesus and the disciples back in the boat. The story has a riddle-like quality—not in the modern sense of a funny-sounding question with an amusing answer, but in the sense of a puzzling exchange. It unfolds as follows:

- ■ The disciples forgot to bring any bread with them in the boat.
- ■ Jesus says, "Watch out—beware of the yeast of the Pharisees and the yeast of Herod." Yeast (leaven) often had a negative connotation in the Jewish world, even as it was also used in everyday life. Here it probably means "contagion," as Jesus warns the disciples to beware of the contagion of the Pharisees and Herod (or Herodians, supporters of Herod Antipas). They have already appeared in combination in Mark 3:6.
- ■ The disciples misunderstand Jesus: though he's talking about yeast, they think he's talking about the fact that they had brought no bread.
- ■ Jesus upbraids them: "Why are you talking about having no bread?"
- ■ He indicts them in sharp accusative language: "Do you still not perceive or understand? Are your hearts hardened? Do you have eyes, and fail to see? Do you have ears, and fail to hear?" Jesus is frustrated that the disciples just

don't "get it"? Do they have hard hearts, he wonders in dismay. Are they blind and deaf?

- Then Jesus asks them how many baskets full of leftovers there were when he fed the five thousand and four thousand. They correctly answer "twelve" and "seven."
- Then Jesus says, "Do you not yet understand?" The story and the section ends.

What are we to make of this? Is it that the disciples couldn't figure out the significance of those numbers? If only they could have seen the meaning of "twelve" and "seven," they would get it? I suspect not. I don't think it's that kind of riddle.

In any case, this section of Mark ends with the disciples, those closest to Jesus, not understanding, not "getting it," just as it began in 6:1–6 with the villagers in Jesus' hometown not "getting it." In the next section of Mark, we'll see that the disciples finally begin to see, even as their seeing remains imperfect.

CHAPTER FOUR

From Galilee to Jerusalem: Mark 8:22–10:52

Mark's gospel begins to move toward Jerusalem. This section bridges the story of Jesus' public activity in Galilee to his final week in the traditional capital of his homeland. Its contents are momentous and, as we will see, central to the meaning of Mark's gospel as a whole. They include:

- The first declaration that Jesus is "the Messiah" by one of his followers (Peter)
- The first explicit mention of Jesus' crucifixion and resurrection in Jerusalem, repeated three times for emphasis
- Teaching about "the way" as following Jesus to Jerusalem. For Mark, this is the meaning of discipleship.

Mark frames this section at the beginning and the end with two stories of blind men regaining their sight: a blind man in Bethsaida in Galilee (8:22–26) and a blind man in Jericho on the last stop before Jerusalem (10:46–52). Thus the middle of his gospel is about "seeing"—seeing that following Jesus means following him from Galilee to Jerusalem.

All of this suggests that this section is more than simply a bridge connecting Galilee and Jerusalem. It is not just the middle of Mark, but the center of his story of Jesus and what it means to follow him. Contemporary gospel scholar John Donahue makes this point by comparing the literary structure of Mark to the architecture of a Roman triumphal arch. On its two side panels are sculpted scenes from the story that the arch celebrates. The side panels point to the middle panel above the arch, which is what the story is most centrally about.

So also this section of Mark is the structural center of his gospel. It discloses, reveals, who Jesus is, the destination of his journey in Jerusalem, and what it means to follow him. It is an epiphany of Jesus and "the way."

A Blind Man Sees: 8:22–26

The previous section of Mark ended with the disciples not "getting it." Jesus accuses them of blindness: "Do you have eyes, and fail to see?" (8:18). Thus it's no surprise that this section begins and ends with blind people regaining their sight.

The first story is set on the north shore of the Sea of Galilee in a fishing village named Bethsaida:

> [22] They came to Bethsaida. Some people brought a blind man to him and begged him to touch him. [23] He took the blind man by the hand and led him out of the village; and when he had put saliva on his eyes and laid his hands upon him, he asked him: "Can you see anything?" [24] And the man looked up and said, "I can see people but they look like trees, walking." [25] Then Jesus laid his hands on his eyes again; and he looked intently and his sight was restored, and he saw everything clearly.

Once again, as in the story of the healing of a deaf mute in 7:32–37, Jesus uses physical means: he "put saliva on his eyes and laid his hands on him." Note that the healing occurs in two stages. After the first stage, the blind man says, "I can see people, but they look like trees, walking" (8:24). He sees indistinctly, imperfectly. In the second stage, Jesus laid his hands on the man's eyes again "and he saw everything clearly" (8:25).

The First Recognition that Jesus is the Messiah (8:27–30)

After the story of the blind man of Bethsaida is what is commonly called "Peter's confession at Caesarea Philippi," which is in the far north of Galilee near today's border with Lebanon. It is an important and pivotal point in Mark: for the first time, a follower of Jesus affirms that he is "the Messiah."

> [27] Jesus went on with his disciples to the villages of Caesarea Philippi; and on the way he asked his disciples, "Who do people say that I am?" [28] And they answered him, "John the Baptist; and others, Elijah; and still others, one of the prophets." [29] He asked them, "But who do you say that I am?" Peter answered him, "You are the Messiah." [30] And he sternly ordered them not to tell anyone about him.

Note that there are two stages in the exchange between Jesus and his disciples, just as there were in the healing of the blind man of Bethsaida. In the first stage, Jesus asks, "Who do people say that I am?" The disciples report what others are saying: "John the Baptist; and others, Elijah; and still others, one of the prophets." The passage has occasionally been understood to refer to reincarnation, but that seems unlikely. Rather, it suggests that people were thinking of Jesus as a prophetic figure—like John, Elijah, and the prophets of the Jewish Bible. That would be an impressive status. But it is inadequate: there is more to be said.

In the second stage, Jesus asks, "But who do *you* say that I am?" Peter says, "You are the Messiah." (Reminder: "Messiah" and "Christ" are synonyms, "Messiah" from the Hebrew word and "Christ" from the Greek word.) To be the Messiah is a status greater than being like John, Elijah, or the prophets.

The understanding of what the Messiah would be like was fluid in first-century Judaism; different groups had different expectations. But all who longed for the Messiah agreed on two features: (1) he would be anointed by the Spirit of God and (2) he would be the decisive figure of Israel's history. The Messiah would usher in God's future, which God intended for Israel and the world. The Messiah would be more than "just" another prophet. Peter's confession means: you are the one we have been waiting for—the Messiah, the anointed and promised one of God.

This is one of the climactic texts in Mark's narrative. Up to this point, neither Jesus nor his followers have used any of the "titles" of Jesus familiar to Christians. Though Mark emphatically affirms in the first verse of his gospel that Jesus is the Messiah and the Son of God, this status is not part of Jesus' teaching and message in Mark. Only the "Spirit world" has used such language: at Jesus' baptism, the Spirit of God declared to him, "You are my Son, the Beloved" (1:11); and evil spirits called him "the Holy One of God" (1:24), "the Son of God!" (3:11), "Son of the Most High God" (5:7). But no human voice has yet done so—neither Jesus nor his followers.

Finally, note how the passage ends. In verse 30, Jesus "sternly ordered them not to tell anyone about him." That Jesus is the Messiah is to be kept secret. Scholars refer to this as "the messianic secret." The secret—the message that Jesus is the Messiah and the Son of God—was, according to Mark, not proclaimed by Jesus himself but only after Easter. Rather, the only affirmations that Jesus is the Messiah occur "in private"—in Jesus' vision at his baptism, here in Mark 8:27–30, then in the Transfiguration story (Mark 9:2–8), and finally in his trial by the authorities (Mark 14:61–62). But none of these affirmations is public.

In short, Jesus' identity as the Messiah and Son of God was not part of Jesus' message in Mark. Jesus did not proclaim himself as "the Messiah" or "the Son of God," and did not call people to believe that he was. This realization does not mean that it is wrong for Christians to call Jesus by these titles—after all, that's who he is for us. But it does mean that Jesus' message in our earliest gospel is not about believing a set of statements about him. Rather, his message is about the coming of the kingdom of God, conveyed in stories about exorcisms, teaching, healing, parables, the sea, feeding, conflict, and "the way."

We Are Going to Jerusalem

Immediately after Peter affirms, "You are the Messiah," Jesus speaks for the first time about his fate and destiny in Jerusalem; he tells the disciples he will be killed by the authorities and raised by God. He repeats this warning three times in Mark's central section. The words toll like a death knell.

The warnings appear at roughly one-chapter intervals. Though only the third one explicitly mentions Jerusalem, the location is implicit in all three. Mark's audience—those who listened to this gospel several decades after Jesus' ministry—already knew Jerusalem was the place of Jesus' execution and resurrection, the city where the authorities who ruled his world would kill him.

The first warning:

Then he began to teach them that the Son of Man must undergo great suffering, and be rejected by the elders, the chief priests, and the scribes, and be killed, and after three days rise again. (8:31)

The second is the briefest:

He was teaching his disciples, saying to them, "The Son of Man is to be betrayed into human hands, and they will kill him, and three days after being killed, he will rise again." (9:31)

The third is the longest and most detailed:

10[32] They were on the road, going up to Jerusalem, and Jesus was walking ahead of them; they were amazed, and those who followed were afraid. He took the twelve aside again and began to tell them what was to happen to him, [33] saying, "See, we are going up to Jerusalem, and the Son of Man will be handed over to the chief priests and the scribes, and they will condemn him to death; then they will hand him over to the Gentiles; [34] they will mock him, and spit upon him, and flog him, and kill him; and after three days he will rise again.

Note that the third passage mentions two sets of authorities, temple and imperial—the chief priests and their scribes will condemn Jesus to death, then hand him over to "the Gentiles" (Roman authority), who will kill him.

The text accurately presents the way Rome ruled the southern part of the Jewish homeland. Beginning in 6 C.E., Judea and Jerusalem were administered by a Roman governor who delegated authority over "internal" and "domestic" Jewish matters to the temple authorities, headed by the high priest. The high priest—chosen from among "the chief priests"—was appointed by the Roman governor. His term of service depended on how well he collaborated with Roman imperial rule. As we will see in the next chapter on Mark's story of Jesus' final week, temple authority and Roman authority collaborated to kill him.

Warning, Misunderstanding, Teaching about the Way

Jesus issues a series of warnings; each is part of a larger threefold pattern: he warns the disciples about what will happen in Jerusalem, they don't get it, and then Jesus teaches about what following him means.

MARK 8:31-37

Immediately after Jesus says for the first time that his path leads to Jerusalem and death, Mark tells us that Peter "took him aside and began to rebuke him." Though Peter has just called Jesus the Messiah, he does not yet see or accept where this is leading. Then:

> ³³ But turning and looking at his disciples, Jesus rebuked Peter and said, "Get behind me, Satan! For you are setting your mind not on divine things but on human things."

Jesus' response is harsh. Calling Peter "Satan," he insists that what Peter is suggesting—that Jesus avoid confrontation and death in Jerusalem—is satanic. Then Jesus turns to the crowd along with his disciples and speaks about what it means to follow him:

> ³⁴ He called the crowd with his disciples, and said to them, "If any want to become my followers, let them deny themselves and take up their cross and follow me."

The language of "followers" and "follow" connects back to the image of "the way" that Mark announced in his overture. Those who would follow Jesus must "take up their cross" and follow him to Jerusalem.

In the first century, taking up one's cross was not yet a broad metaphor for bearing whatever hardship comes one's way, as it has become since. For example, we sometimes speak of a person's cross in life as a difficult in-law or a chronic disease. Rather, in the time of Jesus, "the cross" meant crucifixion, a Roman form of execution designed specifically for those who defied imperial authority. It was not used for "ordinary" criminals such as thieves and murderers. Though they were often executed, they would not be crucified.

Crucifixion was reserved for treason. As a particularly painful, prolonged, and public form of execution, it was a powerful deterrent that sent the message, "This is what we do to those who defy the Roman Empire." In the world of Jesus and early Christianity, a cross was always a Roman cross. The verse about taking up one's cross is amplified in 8:35–37 by sayings about saving and losing one's life:

> 35 For those who want to save their life will lose it, and those who lose their life for my sake, and for the sake of the gospel, will save it. 36 For what will it profit them to gain the whole world and forfeit their life? 37 Indeed, what can they give in return for their life?

The way of the cross is about life and death; to avoid it in order to save one's life is to lose one's life, and to embrace it is to save one's life. The path of death is the path of life.

MARK 9:31–35

The pattern of warning, misunderstanding, and teaching about the way is repeated in the second and briefest anticipation of Jesus' death and resurrection (9:31). The disciples "did not understand what he was saying" (9:32), and they argue with one another "on the way" about which of them was "the greatest." They seem to have missed the point completely. So Jesus presents another lesson:

> 35 He sat down, called the twelve, and said to them, "Whoever wants to be first must be last of all and servant of all."

Again Jesus uses paradoxical language, as in the previous passage about losing one's life in order to save it and saving one's life by losing it. A paradox is a statement that seems contradictory or absurd but expresses a possible truth. Here Jesus says that to be "first" one must be "last" and "servant of all," which is similar in meaning to another paradoxical saying of Jesus, "All who exalt themselves will be humbled and those who humble themselves will be exalted" (Luke 14:11, see also Luke 18:14 and Matt 23:12). To exalt one's self is to puff oneself up; to humble one's self is to empty oneself. In much the

Paradox: a statement affirming what seem to be opposites

same way, to be "the greatest" one must become a servant—or a slave, as the Greek word can also be translated. The path—the way of following Jesus—is not about becoming masters, but servants.

MARK 10:32–45

The threefold pattern appears at greatest length in the third warning of Jesus' destiny in Jerusalem. After the detailed warning in 10:32–34, quoted on page 75, disciples James and John ask Jesus for a favor: "Grant us to sit, one at your right hand and one at your left, in your glory" (10:37). They still haven't "gotten it." They still think that the reward for following Jesus is about greatness.

So Jesus corrects their misunderstanding, using the language of "drinking the cup" and being "baptized," images of dying and death in early Christianity. In Mark 14:36, on the last night of his historical life, Jesus refers to his coming death as "this cup," and Paul's letter to the Romans (6:3–4) refers to baptism as dying (and rising) with Christ.

> [38] Jesus said to them, "You do not know what you are asking. Are you able to drink the cup that I drink, or be baptized with the baptism that I am baptized with?"

When James and John insist that they are able to do so, Jesus offers them a glimpse of what this entails:

> [39] Jesus said to them, "The cup that I drink you will drink; and with the baptism with which I am baptized, you will be baptized; but to sit at my right hand or at my left is not mine to grant, but it is for those for whom it has been prepared."

Following him is the path of drinking the cup and being baptized with his baptism, Jesus tells James and John. The way is about going with Jesus to Jerusalem, the place of dying and rising. Jesus offers his followers not greatness or privilege, but death and resurrection.

Then Jesus calls all of the disciples together and says,

> [42] You know that among the Gentiles those whom they recognize as their rulers lord it over them, and their great ones are tyrants over them. [43] But it is not so among you; but whoever wishes to become great among you must be your servant, [44] and whoever wishes to be first among you must be slave of all.

The third repetition of the pattern is complete and echoes the language of greatness and servant/slave used in the previous instance. Among the Gentiles, "their rulers lord it over them, and their great ones are tyrants." That is the way of domination and tyranny, but it is not to be so among Jesus' followers. Rather, "whoever wishes to become great among you must be your servant. And whoever wishes to be first among you must be slave [servant] of all."

Then, as we've already learned, this passage is followed by the healing of blind Bartimaeus who "regained his sight and followed Jesus on *the way*." *The way* of Jesus leads to Jerusalem—to the cross and resurrection.

What Is the Death and Resurrection of Jesus About?

Christians are familiar with the claim that Jesus' death was of great significance. But why? For close to a thousand years, the most common form of Christianity has spoken of his death as a dying for the sins of the world. Jesus' death has been understood as payment or compensation for human sinfulness: his crucifixion paid the price for our sins so that we can be forgiven. This understanding is known as "substitutionary atonement" or as "substitutionary sacrifice"—a concept that was first fully developed by a bishop and theologian named Anselm of Canterbury in 1097.

> **Substitutionary atonement or substitutionary sacrifice:** seeing Jesus' death as "payment" for our sins—that Jesus died "in our place"

But this concept is not in Mark or in early Christianity. Note that the three warnings of Jesus' fate in Jerusalem do not say, "I must go to Jerusalem *in order to die for the sins of the world*." Rather, they say that Jesus will be *killed by the authorities* who ruled his world. The notion that Jesus died in our place as a substitutionary sacrifice for sin required by God is foreign to Mark and to the other gospels as well.

Only one verse in Mark is sometimes cited to support the notion of substitutionary sacrifice. It occurs at the end of the third repetition of the pattern: "For the Son of Man came not to be served but to serve, and to give his life as a ransom for many" (10:45). But the word "ransom" belongs to the metaphor of liberation from slavery: a "ransom" is the price paid to liberate slaves. Jesus' death is seen as a means of liberation for others.

Importantly, the three warnings do not simply speak of the death of Jesus but also affirm that he will be raised by God. The powers will say "No" to him and kill him—but God will say "Yes" to Jesus and raise him. To follow Jesus is to follow him on the way to death and resurrection in Jerusalem.

In the Gospel Jerusalem has a twofold significance. On the one hand, death and resurrection is one of the New Testament's most central images for the path of personal transformation. Though taking up one's cross could refer to literal martyrdom (some of Jesus' followers were executed in the next several decades and indeed for a few centuries), it had a metaphorical meaning as well. It referred to the spiritual and psychological transformation at the center of following Jesus—dying to an old identity and being born into a new one, dying to an old way of being and being born into a new way of being.

This is the way Luke understands Mark's meaning. As he incorporates Mark 8:34 into his own gospel, he adds the word "daily" (Luke 9:23), suggesting that this transformation is a repeated process, not a one-time martyrdom. Paul the Apostle, too, has a similar understanding: he says about himself, "I have been crucified with Christ, and it is no longer I who live, but it is Christ who lives in me" (Gal. 2:19b–20a). He doesn't mean that he has been literally crucified, but that his old self has died and a new Paul has been born whose identity is now "in Christ."

Following Jesus "on the way" that leads to Jerusalem also has a second meaning. Consider the language of Jesus being "killed." Jesus didn't just die in Jerusalem—he was executed. Jerusalem is the place of confrontation with the powers that ruled Jesus' world. The gospel of the kingdom of God is not simply about personal transformation, essential as that is. It is also about saying "No" to the domination system that killed Jesus. This is the political meaning of following Jesus. The way means standing against the status quo in the name of Jesus' passion for the kingdom of God—what life would be like on earth if God were king and the rulers of this world were not.

All of this is quite different from the idea that Jesus' death was a substiutionary sacrifice for sin—the notion means that Jesus died for us so that we don't have to. For Mark, following Jesus to Jerusalem means participating in his death and resurrection. Rather than substitutionary atonement, Mark speaks of participatory atonement. We are called not simply to believe that Jesus has done it for us, but to participate in his passion. That is the way of becoming "at one" with God.

> **Participatory atonement:** we become reconciled to God by participating in Jesus' path of death and resurrection

We will see the confrontation between Jesus and the religious and imperial authorities in more detail in the next chapter. Now we turn to other topics in the great central section of Mark.

The Transfiguration: 9:2–8

Between the first and second anticipations of what will happen in Jerusalem is the story of the transfiguration of Jesus. Three of Jesus' disciples ascend a high mountain with him and there they see Jesus transfigured, his body and clothes filled with light—dazzling, unearthly white. It is an experience of Jesus filled with the glory—the radiant luminosity—of God. Two of the greatest figures of Israel's history appear with Jesus:

> [2] Jesus took with him Peter and James and John, and led them up a high mountain apart, by themselves. And he was transfigured before them, [3] and his clothes became dazzling white, such as no one on earth could bleach them. [4] And there appeared to them Elijah with Moses, who were talking with Jesus. [5] Then Peter said to Jesus, "Rabbi, it is good for us to be here; let us make three dwellings, one for you, one for Moses, and one for Elijah." [6] He did not know what to say, for they were terrified.

Then the same voice that had spoken to Jesus at his baptism speaks to the three disciples, *the bath qol*, the daughter of a sound: "A cloud overshadowed them, and from the cloud there came a voice, 'This is my Son, the Beloved; listen to him!'" (9:7). The voice of God that said to Jesus at his baptism, "*You* are my Son, the Beloved" (1:11) now speaks directly to the inner three of his followers: "*This* is my Son. Listen to him!" What are Peter, James, and John to listen to, to hear? The answer is found in the theme of this section: Jesus is going to Jerusalem where he will be killed by the authorities and raised by God. Listen to him—follow him.

As they come down from the mountain, the messianic secret is re-affirmed. Jesus "ordered them to tell no one about what they had seen, until after the Son of Man had risen from the dead" (9:9). According to Mark, Jesus' identity and status as the Son of God is a post-Easter proclamation.

Teaching about Wealth

Near the middle of Mark's central section are some difficult sayings—about the incompatibility between being wealthy and entering the kingdom of God.

First is the story about a rich man who wishes to follow Jesus in 10:17–22. Though often called "the story of the rich young ruler," Mark says only that he was wealthy ("he had many possessions"). That he was young comes from Matthew's version of the story and that he was a ruler comes from Luke (Matt 19:22, Luke 18:18).

> [17] As he was setting out on a journey, a man ran up and knelt before him, and asked him, "Good Teacher, what must I do to inherit eternal life?" [18] Jesus said to him, "Why do you call me good? No one is good but God alone. [19] You know the commandments: You shall not murder; You shall not commit adultery; You shall not steal; You shall not bear false witness; You shall not defraud; Honor your father and mother." [20] He said to him, "Teacher, I have kept all these since my youth." [21] Jesus, looking at him, loved him and said, "You lack one thing; go, sell what you own, and give the money to the poor, and you will have treasure in heaven; then come, follow." [22] When he heard this, he was shocked and went away grieving, for he had many possessions.

It is natural for us to imagine that this man is asking Jesus what he must do to get to heaven, for that is what the phrase "eternal life" has come to mean to many Christians. But the Greek phrase used by Mark renders the Jewish notion of "the life of the age to come"—a transformed earth, or the kingdom of God. Not heaven, but God's kingdom on earth.

Jesus' initial response is surprising: "Why do you call me good? No one is good but God alone." His words suggest a difference between Jesus and God that Matthew was uncomfortable with—as he incorporated Mark's story into his gospel, he changed Jesus' question to "Why do you ask me about what is good?" (Matt 19:17).

Jesus responds to the man's question by citing most of the Ten Commandments (if we understand "Do not defraud" as a variation of "Do not covet"). The man replies that he has observed all these laws from his youth. Note that Jesus does not challenge his statement. Instead, looking at him and loving him, Jesus says, "You lack one thing; go, sell what you own, and give the money to the poor, and you will have treasure in heaven," and concludes with the invitation: "Come, follow." Once again, Mark stresses the theme is following Jesus. The life of which Jesus speaks is not just about observing the commandments, but about following him. It is too much for the rich man: "He was shocked and went away grieving, for he had many possessions."

Over the centuries interpreters have often softened this story by suggesting that it applied to this particular rich man—that Jesus had perceived that wealth was the primary preoccupation of his life. But the next few verses generalize the teaching:

> [23] Then Jesus looked around and said to his disciples, "How hard it will be for those who have wealth to enter the kingdom of God!" [24] And the disciples were perplexed at these words. But Jesus said to them again, "Children, how hard it is to enter the kingdom of God! [25] It is easier for a camel to go through the eye of a needle than for someone who is rich to enter the kingdom of God."

Twice Jesus says how hard it will be for those who have wealth to enter the kingdom of God, concluding with the familiar, "It is easier for a camel to go through the eye of a needle than for someone who is rich to enter the kingdom of God." Interpreters have sometimes softened this saying by pointing out that there was a gate in the walls of Jerusalem known as "The Needle Gate" because it was so low that it could be entered only getting down on ones hands and knees—it was difficult to pass through, but not impossible. But this interpretation seems unlikely.

Rather, these sayings are consistent with a repeated emphasis in the gospels. "Wealth" and "the wealthy" are sharply criticized by Jesus:

- ■ "No one can serve two masters. . . . You cannot serve God and wealth" ("mammon": in older translations) (Matt 6:24; see also Luke 16:13)

■ Woes to the rich: immediately following the blessings on the poor and hungry in Luke 6:20–22 is a series of woes addressed to the rich, the full, the laughing, and those who are well regarded (Luke 6:24–26)

■ Parables indicting wealthy people: the Rich Farmer (Luke 12:13–21), the Rich Man and Lazarus (Luke 16:19–31)

These teachings often cause discomfort and are often misunderstood. Many Western Christians are reasonably well off financially, especially compared to the poor in our nations and in the developing world. Is it wrong to be financially comfortable? Are we supposed to feel guilty about it? Do these sayings mean that wealthy people can't be good people? They can often make us squirm in discomfort.

These sayings are also commonly misunderstood. When they are coupled with the common notion that the Christian gospel is about how to get to heaven, the issue becomes, "Can't wealthy people go to heaven?" Then the conversation turns to requirements for salvation beyond death.

But in their first-century historical context, that is not what Jesus' teachings about wealth and the wealthy were about. In his world, the wealthy were part of the ruling elite at the top of the domination system—the wealthiest one to two percent of the population who set the system up so that one-half to two-thirds of the production of wealth from the peasant class flowed to them. In that world, if you were wealthy, you were a collaborator with the domination system or at least complicit with it.

The issue was not individual virtue. Wealthy people, then as now, could be good people as individuals—after all, Jesus does not question the rich man's statement that he has observed all the commandments from his youth. Individual goodness was not the issue, but the complicity of the wealthy in a system that radically impoverished the peasant class. The alternative was the kingdom of God.

So as we think about what these teachings mean for us now, it is illuminating to begin with what they meant then. "No one can serve two masters" was initially a comment about the wealthy in the historical world of Jesus. Wealth and indifference to the suffering caused by it went together. And, of course, the same is true in our world: wealth can easily become a preoccupation, a snare, a "cage."

A personal comment: don't feel guilty if your life has turned out well financially. Be grateful—it is something to be thankful for. But do ponder what it might mean to take seriously God's passion for a transformed world—the kingdom of God—as seen in Jesus. The question for those of us who have some wealth then becomes: how do we use the wealth we have been given to further God's passion for a different kind of world?

The Coming of the Son of Man and the Kingdom of God

This section also includes a passage that refers to the coming of "the Son of Man" and the kingdom of God in the near future. In Mark 8:38–9:1, Jesus says:

> [38] "Those who are ashamed of me and of my words in this adulterous and sinful generation, of them the Son of Man will also be ashamed when he comes in the glory of his Father with the holy angels." [1] And he said to them "Truly I tell you, there are some standing here who will not taste death until they see that the kingdom of God has come with power."

Until now in Mark, the phrase "the Son of Man" has been used to refer to Jesus in his present activity (see, for example, Mark 2:10, 28; and in the three warnings of what will happen in Jerusalem). But this passage refers to a future judgment when "the Son of Man . . . comes in the glory of his Father with the holy angels." The next verse links this event to the coming of the kingdom of God and implies that it will happen soon: some of those standing there will not die before they see "that the kingdom of God has *come with power.*"

Though other suggestions are sometimes made, this passage is most plausibly understood as referring to the second coming of Jesus. At least some early Christians expected it to happen soon; see, for example, Paul in 1 Thessalonians 4:13–18, 1 Corinthians 15:51–52, Romans 13:11–12. In the book of Revelation, the second coming of Jesus is affirmed seven times to be "soon," "near," and later in the gospel of Mark, he writes about it too. The climax of Mark 13 speaks of the coming of "'the Son of Man in clouds' with great power and glory," foretelling that this would happen in "this generation":

> [24] But in those days, after that suffering, the sun will be darkened, and the moon will not give its light, [25] and the stars will be falling from heaven, and the powers in the heavens will be shaken. [26] Then they will see 'the Son of Man coming in clouds' with great power and glory. [27] Then he will send out the angels, and gather his elect from the four winds, from the ends of the earth to the ends of heaven. [28] From the fig tree learn its lesson: as soon as its branch becomes tender and puts forth its leaves, you know that summer is near. [29] So also, when you see these things taking place, you know that he is near, at the very gates: [30] Truly I tell you, this generation will not pass away until all these things have taken place.

The technical term for this expectation is "imminent eschatology"—the conviction that the *eschaton* (a Greek word meaning "the end") is near. Importantly, within the Jewish world of Jesus, "the end" is not about the end of the world as the physical universe but about the transformation of the humanly created world of injustice and violence and the coming of the kingdom of God. *Imminent eschatology* means "it will be soon." Imminent eschatology also includes the notion that this transformation will be brought about through divine intervention: if it's going to happen soon, it can only happen through an act of God. God will do it.

Imminent eschatology: the belief that God will intervene soon in a dramatic way to transform the world

Mark expected this—and he was wrong. Scholars are divided about whether this expectation goes back to Jesus or whether it is the product of the early Christian movement in the decades after Jesus' death. My own probability judgment is the latter. Indeed, Mark's historical context as a wartime gospel written around the year 70 may explain his emphasis on the nearness of the coming of the Son of Man and the kingdom in power. Given the significance of Jerusalem as the center of the Jewish world and its temple as the place of God's presence, their destruction (whether imminent or having just occurred) may well have intensified the expectation that God would soon intervene against the powers that ravaged the world.

Seeing and Following the Way: Mark 10:46–52

Just as this section of Mark began with one blind man receiving his sight, so it ends with another. In 10:46–52, as Jesus and his followers leave Jericho and are about to begin the last stage of their journey to Jerusalem, they encounter a blind beggar named Bartimaeus:

> [46] They came to Jericho. As he and his disciples and a large crowd were leaving Jericho, Bartimaeus son of Timaeus, a blind beggar, was sitting by the roadside. [47] When he heard that it was Jesus of Nazareth, he began to shout out and say, "Jesus, Son of David, have mercy on me!" [48] Many sternly ordered him to be quiet, but he cried out even more loudly, "Son of David, have mercy on me!" [49] Jesus stood still and said, "Call him here." And they called the blind man, saying to him, "Take heart; get up, he is calling you." [50] So throwing off his cloak, he sprang up and came to Jesus. [51] Then Jesus said to him, "What do you want me to do for you?" The blind man said to him, "My teacher, let me see again." [52] Jesus said to him, "Go; your faith has made you well." Immediately he regained his sight and followed him on the way.

His sight restored, his cloak cast off, Bartimaeus *"followed Jesus on the way."* In the next verse, at the beginning of Mark 11, we arrive in Jerusalem. The way—the theme of this great central section—is following Jesus to Jerusalem. It is the place of death and resurrection.

CHAPTER FIVE

Jerusalem, Execution and Resurrection: Mark 11–16

Mark's story reaches Jerusalem. The importance of Jesus' final week is indicated by the space Mark devotes to it: six chapters, more than a third of his gospel, compared to ten chapters for the whole of Jesus' public activity up to this point. In this section, Mark's narrative slows down and becomes far more detailed, providing a day-by-day account of Jesus' final week. (For a book-length treatment of this part of Mark, see *The Last Week*[5].)

Sunday: The Entry into Jerusalem (11:1–10)

Jesus and those following him on "the way" arrive in Jerusalem at the beginning of the week of Passover, the most important of the three annual Jewish pilgrimage festivals. It remembered and celebrated the exodus from bondage to the Egyptian Empire over a thousand years earlier. It was (and is) to Judaism what Holy Week is to Christians: the most sacred time of the year.

At Passover, more people gathered in Jerusalem than at any other time. Estimates of the population in the first century are about forty thousand. But at Passover, as many as two hundred thousand to three hundred thousand Jewish pilgrims would flood the city.

On the first day of Passover—known to Christians as Palm Sunday—Jesus and his followers reach the top of the Mount of Olives overlooking Jerusalem from the east. Then Jesus rides a donkey down the mountain and enters the city at the head of a procession of his followers.

Passover: Jewish festival celebrating the exodus from Egypt

To see the powerful and provocative meanings of this familiar story, it is important to know that another procession—a Roman imperial procession—was entering Jerusalem for Passover, possibly on the same day. Though Mark does not mention the Roman procession, he and his community would have known about it, as would Jesus and his followers earlier in the first century. Each Passover, the Roman governor of Judea came to Jerusalem from the Mediterranean coastal city of Caesarea Maritima, the capital of Roman provincial administration. He did so because of the incendiary potential of the Jewish festival: more than once it had been the occasion for anti-Roman riots and revolts.

And so the Roman governor Pontius Pilate came to Jerusalem at the beginning of that Passover. Of course, he did not come alone. Entering the city from the west, he was accompanied by imperial troops and cavalry to reinforce the Roman garrison permanently stationed in a fortress next to the temple and its courts. The imperial procession represented, both actually and symbolically, Roman economic and political domination of the Jewish homeland through military power and the threat of its use.

This is the context for seeing what Jesus' entry means. As Mark tells the story at the beginning of chapter 11:

> [1] When they were approaching Jerusalem, at Bethphage and Bethany, near the Mount of Olives, he sent two of his disciples [2] and said to them, "Go into the village ahead of you, and immediately as you enter it, you will find tied there a colt that has never been ridden; untie it and bring it. [3] If anyone says to you, 'Why are you doing this?' just say this, 'The Lord needs it and will send it back here immediately.'" [4] They went away and found a colt tied near a door, outside in the street. As they were untying it, [5] some of the bystanders said to them, "What are you doing,

untying the colt?" [6] They told them what Jesus had said; and they allowed them to take it.

Jesus has made elaborate pre-arrangements. His riding into the city on a colt is not incidental or accidental, but deliberate and intentional. As my mentor George Caird wrote over forty years ago, this is a pre-planned public demonstration.

> [7] Then they brought the colt to Jesus and threw their cloaks on it; and he sat on it. [8] Many people spread their cloaks on the road, and others spread leafy branches that they had cut in the fields. [9] Then those who went ahead and those who followed were shouting, "Hosanna! Blessed is the one who comes in the name of the Lord! [10] Blessed is the coming kingdom of our ancestor David! Hosanna in the highest heaven!"

Note the kingdom language at the end of the passage, as Jesus' followers chant: "Blessed is the one who comes in the name of the Lord, blessed is the coming *kingdom* of our ancestor David." What does this story of Jesus intentionally, deliberately, riding into Jerusalem on a colt mean? The answer is provided by a text from the Jewish Bible, the Christian Old Testament. Zechariah 9:9–10 speaks of a future king who will ride into Jerusalem on the colt of a donkey. He will banish the weapons of war from the land—chariots, war horses, and battle bows—and speak peace to the nations. (Matthew makes the connection even more plain by quoting Zechariah 9:9 as he incorporates Mark's story into his gospel in Matthew 21:4–5.)

The point is not that Zechariah predicted Jesus' entry into Jerusalem but that Jesus intentionally enacted the passage from Zechariah: it was a symbolic act, performed for its meaning. Some of the prophets of the Old Testament performed such acts to symbolize their message. This act of Jesus stands in that tradition.

As a public symbolic act, it was both protest and affirmation. As protest, it was an anti-Roman act, for Rome was the empire that ruled the land with the instruments of war. As affirmation, it symbolized a different vision of life on earth: the kingdom of God of which Jesus spoke, and which his followers heralded as he rode into the city. That kingdom is about peace and non-violence—not just internal peace, but the alternative to domination systems imposed by violence and the threat of violence.

The contrast between the two processions—of Jesus and the Romans—embodies the central conflict of the week between Jesus, who proclaimed the kingdom of God, and the religious and political authorities, who were in charge of the domination system. Before the end of the week, they will kill him.

Monday: The Disruption in the Temple (11:15–19)

Jesus and the disciples do not stay in Jerusalem, but travel back to the village of Bethany to spend Sunday night (11:11). On Monday they return to the city and go to the temple. There Jesus performs another public demonstration, another symbolic act: he overturns the tables of moneychangers and sellers of sacrificial doves:

> [15] Then they came to Jerusalem. And he entered the temple and began to drive out those who were selling and those who were buying in the temple, and he overturned the tables of the money changers and the seats of those who sold doves.

The act occurred not in the temple building itself, but in one of the temple courts that had been built by Herod the Great in his expansion of the temple area that began some years before Jesus' birth. Herod created a massive temple platform, a flat area about 1500 feet long and 900 feet wide. He surrounded it with porticoes—roofed structures supported by marble columns. Herod's reconstruction of the temple and its courts created one of the most impressive structures in the Roman world. Not only Jews but also Gentiles were awed by its beauty, size, and elegance.

In one of these courts, there were money-changers and sellers of sacrificial animals who provided a service to Jewish pilgrims traveling from a distance. The annual temple tax had to be paid in a particular kind of silver coin, and the money-changers were there to change coins into the appropriate coinage. So also the sellers of sacrificial animals sold pilgrims the animals they needed to provide for sacrifice.

There was nothing illicit or corrupt about this. We know from Jewish sources that rates of exchange and prices of animals were rigorously regulated. So the issue was not that such selling should not have been happening in the temple courts, or that the merchants were fleecing the pilgrims. So what did Jesus' act mean? Mark tells us in the teaching that accompanies this passage. After the overturning of the tables, Jesus said:

> ¹⁷ "Is it not written, 'My house shall be called a house of prayer for all the nations'? But you have made it a den of robbers."

The quotation combines two phrases from the Old Testament. The first phrase—"My house shall be called a house of prayer for all the nations"—is from Isaiah 56:7, where "my house" refers to the temple. Prayer, Jesus insists, is the purpose of God's temple.

The second phrase—"a den of robbers"—comes from Jeremiah 7:11 and speaks of what the temple has become. In the context of Jeremiah 7:1–15, one of Jeremiah's temple indictments, the meaning is clear: it refers to the rulers of Jerusalem, the monarchy and the temple, who practice injustice, oppress the vulnerable (widows, orphans, and aliens), shed innocent blood, and yet think that they are safe because they worship God in the temple. That is why Jeremiah calls the temple "a den of robbers." The phrase has nothing to do with merchants overcharging pilgrims.

Jesus' use of the phrase from Jeremiah suggests a similar meaning. As in the time of Jeremiah, the temple had become "a den of robbers"—the center of religious collaboration with Roman imperial rule. That prevented the temple from being what it was meant to be—a house of prayer for all the nations.

The temple authorities understood this:

> ¹⁸ And when the chief priests and the scribes heard it, they kept looking for a way to kill him; for they were afraid of him, because the whole crowd was spellbound by his teaching.

They want to kill Jesus but are stymied by the crowd of pilgrims surrounding him, so they do not dare to arrest him. At the end of the day, Jesus and his followers once again leave the city, probably heading back to the village of Bethany.

Finally, note that Mark frames Jesus' actions in the temple with the story of the cursing of a fig tree (11:12–14, 20–24)—another example of Mark's sandwich technique (recall, for example, 5:24–34 framed by 5:21–23 and 5:35–43, treated in Chapter 2). On Monday morning as Jesus makes his way to the temple, hungry, he sees a fig tree, but there are no figs on it, so he curses it. The next morning as Jesus and his disciples once again return to the city, the fig tree has "withered away to its roots" (11:20).

The story has puzzled many Christians. Why would Jesus curse a tree—especially when figs weren't even in season? As a factual narrative, the story makes little sense. But as a parabolic story, it does: the temple has not been producing the fruit it should have, so the withering of the fig tree symbolizes what the the temple had become.

In all of these stories, do not hear an indictment of Judaism. Judaism was not the problem. The problem was the imperial captivity of the temple and its authorities' collaboration with the Empire. For Jesus, the solution was an alternative tradition of Judaism. Thus the anti-imperial entry on Sunday is strikingly consistent with the anti-temple act on Monday.

Tuesday: Conflict with Temple Authorities (11:27–13:2)

Jesus and his disciples return to Jerusalem on Tuesday. As Mark tells the story, it is a busy day. In the courts of the temple, filled with pilgrims ("the crowd"), representatives of the religious authorities seek to discredit Jesus but are consistently confounded.

- In 11:27–33, chief priests, scribes, and elders challenge Jesus: "By what authority are you doing things?" (11:28). Jesus offers them a deal: if they will tell him by what authority John baptized, he will tell them by what authority he is doing these things. They realize that if they say that John's authority came from God, Jesus will ask them why they rejected him. But if they say John's authority was of human origin, the crowd will turn against them. So they lamely reply, "We do not know" (11:33). Fair enough, Jesus says: you haven't answered my question so I won't answer yours.
- In 12:1–12, Jesus tells a parable, commonly called "The Parable of the Wicked Tenants." A man plants a vineyard with great care and leases it to tenants. When the harvest comes, he sends

a series of servants to collect his share of the produce. But the tenants beat them, send them away empty-handed, and even kill one of them. So the owner of the vineyard finally sends his son, but the tenants kill him too. Then Jesus asks, "What then will the owner of the vineyard do?" He provides the obvious answer: "He will come and destroy the tenants and give the vineyard to others" (12:9). The text ends at 12:12, with the representatives of the authorities realizing "that he had told this parable against them." They want to arrest him, but still fear the crowd.

■ In 12:13–17, Herodians and Pharisees ask Jesus a loaded question: Is it lawful to pay taxes to Caesar? We treat this passage in greater detail, in part to illustrate the brilliance of Jesus' responses in these conflict stories, and also because of its importance in subsequent Christian history.

[13] Then they sent to him some Pharisees and some Herodians to trap him in what he said. [14] And they came and said to him, "Teacher, we know that you are sincere, and show deference to no one; for you do not regard people with partiality, but teach the way of God in accordance with truth. Is it lawful to pay taxes to the emperor, or not? [15] Should we pay them, or should we not?" But knowing their hypocrisy, he said to them, "Why are you putting me to the test? Bring me a denarius and let me see it." [16] And they brought one. Then he said to them, "Whose head is this, and whose title?" They answered, "The emperor's." [17] Jesus said to them, "Give to the emperor the things that are the emperor's, and to God the things that are God's."

Note the purpose of the questioners, identified as "some Pharisees and some Herodians," is to "trap him." They begin by flattering Jesus and then ask about the lawfulness of paying taxes to the emperor.

Why is this question a trap? Because answering either yes or no would get Jesus in trouble. Paying taxes to Rome was accepted by the temple authorities (indeed, they were responsible for collecting them) but resented by many Jews, not simply because of the money involved but also because it was a sign of Jewish submission to imperial rule. So if Jesus said "yes," he risked alienating many of the crowd of pilgrims. Indeed, his interrogators hoped to do this, for if they could turn the crowd against Jesus, then they could arrest him. On the other hand, if Jesus said "no," that would be explicit encouragement to reject Roman rule—nothing less than treason and sedition.

Note the brilliance of Jesus' response. Rather than answering the question, he deflects it by asking them if they have a *denarius* and to bring it to him. That Jesus asks for a *denarius* is significant, for it was a Roman coin that had the image of Caesar on it (there were other coins in circulation in the Jewish homeland that did not have images on them). They do so, and already they have discredited themselves with the crowd: they are carrying coins bearing images, prohibited by Jewish law.

Denarius: the smallest Roman silver coin; a day's wage in the peasant class

Then, so the whole crowd can hear, Jesus asks them, "Whose head is this, and whose title?" The head, of course, is Caesar, and the inscription contained titles of Caesar, among which was "Son of God." They answer—rather sheepishly, we may imagine—"The emperor's." Then Jesus says, "Give to the emperor the things that are the emperor's, and to God the things that are God's." It's Caesar's coin—give it back to him.

Christians have often understood this to be an affirmative answer to the question about taxes to Caesar—as if there are two realms, one political and one religious, and that taxes are to be paid to political authorities and religious devotion offered to God. Many American Christians see this verse as the biblical basis of separation between church and state.

But this is not what the passage meant. In its context, Jesus was not making a doctrinal statement about the distinction between political and religious obligation. He was simultaneously evading a trap and turning the trap against hostile interrogators. Moreover, imagine that Jesus had been asked a follow-up question: what belongs to the emperor and what belongs to God? Given all that we know about him, it seems clear that his answer would have been, "Everything belongs to God—nothing belongs to the emperor."

We continue our summary of Tuesday:

- In 12:18–27, Sadducees (an aristocratic group allied with the chief priests) interrogate Jesus about an afterlife, seeking to show that the notion is ridiculous.

- In 12:28–34, a scribe asks Jesus about the greatest commandment. Jesus' response in 12:29–31 combines verses from Deuteronomy 6:4–5 and Leviticus 19:18: "The first is, 'Hear, O Israel: the Lord our God, the Lord is one; you shall love the Lord your God with all your heart, and with all your soul, and with all your mind, and with all your strength.' The second is this, 'You shall love your neighbor as yourself.' There is no other commandment greater than these."

> **Sadducees:** a wealthy Jewish group associated with the higher ranks of the priesthood

- In 12:35–37, Jesus asks a "riddle" about the Messiah and the Son of David.
- In 12:38–40, Jesus indicts scribes (a literate class who worked for the authorities) who "devour widow's houses," presumably by foreclosure for debt.
- In 12:41–44, Jesus praises the devotion of a poor widow and contrasts her generosity to the actions of the wealthy.
- In 13:1–2, Jesus warns that the temple will be destroyed.

Still Tuesday: "The Little Apocalypse" (13:3–37)

Immediately following the warning of the temple's destruction is Mark's "little apocalypse," called that because its subject matter is similar to "the big apocalypse"—the book of Revelation. This passage is about "the end" and signs that it is near. As we learned in Mark 8:38—9:1, Mark expected this soon, perhaps because of the momentous events of the year 70, when Jerusalem and the temple were conquered and destroyed by the Romans. According to Mark 13:

- There will be false messiahs, wars, rumors of wars, nations and kingdoms rising against nations and kingdoms, earthquakes, and famines; these are but "the beginnings of the birth pangs" (verses 5–8).
- Jesus' followers will be persecuted by councils and synagogues, governors and kings. There will be betrayals (verses 9–13).
- There will be a "desolating sacrilege." The phrase echoes the book of Daniel and refers to Jerusalem and its temple desolated

by a pagan empire. This will be a time of great suffering and more false messiahs (verses 14–23).

■ Then "the sun will be darkened and the moon will not give its light, and the stars will be falling from heaven, and the powers in the heavens will be shaken." When this happens, "they will see the Son of Man coming in clouds with great power and glory." He "will send out the angels, and gather his elect from the four winds, from the ends of the earth to the ends of heaven" (verses 24–27).

■ All of this, the Jesus of Mark says, will take place soon: "Truly I tell you, this generation will not pass away until all these things have taken place" (verse 30).

As we also saw in our comments on Mark 8:38–9:1, scholars are divided about whether to attribute the imminent coming of "the Son of Man in clouds with great power and glory" to Jesus or to his post-Easter followers. Recall that the authors of the gospels all wrote near or after the events of 70. In either case, it is important to know that passages in the Bible can be wrong. To say the obvious, though Jerusalem and the temple were destroyed, the coming of "the Son of Man in clouds with great power and glory" did not happen.

Wednesday: Anointing for Burial and Betrayal (14:1–11)

Mark's account of Wednesday is brief. Two things happen. The first involves temple authorities and their desire to arrest and kill Jesus. In Mark 14:1–2, "the chief priests and the scribes" are "looking for a way to arrest Jesus *by stealth* and kill him." They do not dare to move against him in the presence of the crowd for fear of a riot. But as Wednesday ends, their problem is solved: Judas, one of Jesus' disciples, comes to them and offers to betray him by telling them where they can find Jesus apart from the crowd (14:10–11).

In between those two events is the story of Jesus' body being anointed for burial. He is in Bethany, the village near but outside Jerusalem where he and his disciples have returned each night. There is a gathering for a meal in the house of Simon the leper—recall that lepers were an untouchable class, outcasts. As the story unfolds, the main character is an unnamed woman:

³ While he was at Bethany in the house of Simon the leper, as he sat at the table, a woman came with an alabaster jar of very costly ointment of nard, and she broke open the jar and poured the ointment on his head. ⁴ But some were there who said to one another in anger, "Why was the ointment wasted in this way? ⁵ For this ointment could have been sold for more than three hundred denarii, and the money given to the poor." And they scolded her.

Some—presumably disciples and other followers of Jesus—object to what this woman has done. Yet they show signs that they have not completely misunderstood what Jesus is about. They know about his passion for the poor. Three hundred *denarii* was a significant amount of money—a *denarius* was the average daily wage in the peasant class, and so three hundred was almost a year's income. But Jesus defends her:

> ⁶ Let her alone; why do you trouble her? She has performed a good service for me. ⁷ For you always have the poor with you, and you can show kindness to them whenever you wish; but you will not always have me. ⁸ She has done what she could; she has anointed my body beforehand for its burial. ⁹ Truly I tell you, wherever the good news [gospel] is proclaimed in the whole world, what she has done will be told in remembrance of her.

A negative comment: the words "you always have the poor with you" have been used by some Christians to justify the persistence of poverty and the impossibility of doing anything about it—that's just the way things are. But to use Jesus, the champion of the peasant class, to legitimate huge differentials of wealth seems rather cynical.

A positive comment: Jesus commends the unnamed woman: "Wherever the good news is proclaimed in the whole world, what she has done will be told in remembrance of her" (verse 9). Why? Because she "gets it." She understands what the rest of Jesus' disciples have not yet understood—that his life is headed for death; he will soon be killed. So she anoints him for burial now, not knowing whether she will have another opportunity to do so.

Thursday: Last Supper, Gethsemane, and Arrest (14:12—52)

Jesus has made plans to celebrate the Passover meal with his followers (14:12–16). It will be his last supper, for he will soon be arrested, condemned, and executed. During the meal, Jesus gives the bread and wine symbolic significance:

> [22] He took a loaf of bread, and after blessing it he broke it, gave it to them, and said, "Take; this is my body." [23] Then he took a cup, and after giving thanks he gave it to them, and all of them drank from it. [24] He said to them, "This is my blood of the covenant, which is poured out for many."

This is Mark's account of what Christians commonly call "the words of institution" of what is variously named as "the Mass," "the Eucharist," "the Lord's Supper," or "communion."

There are other versions of these words in the New Testament. Matthew 26:28 adds "for the forgiveness of sins." Luke 22:19–20 adds after bread/body: "given for you. Do this in remembrance of me."

The words of institution: the words accompanying the eucharist: this is my body, this is my blood

The Apostle Paul's version is also slightly different. In 1 Corinthians 11:23–26 (written in the 50s, before the gospels), Paul reports that Jesus said about the bread: "This is my body that is for you. Do this in remembrance of me." About the wine: "This cup is the new covenant in my blood. Do this, as often you drink it, in remembrance of me."

The different versions of "the words of institution" need not (and do not) create doubt about the importance of Christian observance of Jesus' last supper. Rather, the variations illustrate that the traditions about Jesus developed in differing ways in different early Christian communities.

What they all have in common is a meal in which bread and wine are given special significance: the bread is declared to be Jesus' body, the wine his blood. The language points to a violent death, for only in a violent death are body and blood separated from each other. Soon Jesus will undergo such a death.

To this, Mark adds covenantal language: "This is my blood of the covenant, which is poured out for many." Blood as a means of sealing a covenant goes back to Israel's past. In Exodus 24:1–8, the covenant between God and Israel at Mt. Sinai was sealed with blood dashed upon the people. Now the covenant of which Jesus speaks is sealed with his blood, "poured out for many." Though the words affirm that

Jesus' death will benefit "the many," there is no suggestion that his death is payment for the sins of the many. Sealing a covenant with blood and substitutionary sacrifice are not the same thing.

To complete Mark's narrative of Thursday evening and night:

- At the meal, Jesus says that one of the twelve disciples will betray him (14:17–21). Though this disciple is not named, we readers already know it will be Judas.
- After the meal, Jesus tells Peter that he will deny Jesus and that the other disciples will flee (14:26–31).
- Jesus and the disciples go to a garden on the Mount of Olives where Jesus prays and the disciples fall asleep (14:32–42).
- Soon Judas arrives with armed men sent by the temple authorities to arrest Jesus. The disciples flee (14:43–52).
- Before the night is over, Peter will have denied Jesus three times (14:66–72). Jesus faces his fate alone.

Condemnation, Crucifixion, and Death (14:53—15:47)

We begin with two preliminary comments as we turn to Mark's story of Jesus' death. First, those of us who grew up as Christians, even if only marginally so, bring preconceptions to this story. Many—perhaps most—of us acquired the understanding that Jesus died for—perhaps because of—the sins of the world. For many, Jesus' crucifixion was payment"—a substitutionary sacrifice—for sin.

Note that this understanding also implies that Jesus' death was necessary—that it had to happen, that it was part of God's plan, indeed that God required it. But, as we saw in Chapter 5, this understanding is less than a thousand years old, and it is not found in Mark. So let's set that idea aside as we seek to hear Mark's story. Without this filter, this lens, what does this story mean?

Second, remember that Mark's story of Jesus' condemnation and crucifixion combine memory and metaphor, just as his gospel as a whole does. Memory: Jesus really was executed in Jerusalem at Passover by Roman authority (in that world, a cross was always a Roman cross) with the collaboration of religious authority. Metaphor: as Mark tells the story, he gives it a metaphorical meaning—a more-than-literal, more-than-factual meaning. Some of the details may be purely metaphorical—that is, included for their meaning, not because of their factuality.

Condemnation by Collaborationist Religious Authority (14:53–65)

This portion of the story is sometimes referred to as "the Jewish trial of Jesus." The language is misleading. It may not have been a "trial" in the literal sense of the word. Scholars have correctly noted that what happens does not conform to Jewish laws concerning trials. And the phrase "the Jewish trial" implies that it was "the Jews" who rejected Jesus. But as Mark tells the story, it is not "the Jews" who take the lead, but the temple authorities. As you read the story, note that they, collaborators with Roman imperial rule, are the ones who are mentioned:

> [53] They took Jesus to **the high priest; and all the chief priests, the elders, and the scribes** were assembled. [54] Peter had followed him at a distance, right into the courtyard of the high priest; and he was sitting with the guards, warming himself at the fire. [55] Now **the chief priests and the whole council** were looking for testimony against Jesus to put him to death; but they found none. [56] For many gave false testimony against him, and their testimony did not agree. [57] Some stood up and gave false testimony against him, saying, [58] "We heard him say, 'I will destroy this temple that is made with hands, and in three days I will build another, not made with hands.'" [59] But even on this point their testimony did not agree.

The accusation—that Jesus said that he would "destroy this temple that is made with hands, and in three days I will build another, not made with hands"—is a garbled version of something that, according to Mark, Jesus had done and said. In the anti-temple act on Monday and in Mark 13:2, Jesus had threatened the temple with destruction because it had become "a den of robbers." But did he say, "*I* will destroy this temple made with hands"? Was he bent on violence? Note that the testimony of the accusers does not agree.

In the absence of two or three witnesses who confirm each other's testimony, the high priest goes for a confession:

> [60] Then the high priest stood up before them and asked Jesus, "Have you no answer? What is it that they testify against you?" [61] But he was silent and did not answer. Again the high priest asked him, "Are you the Messiah, the Son of the Blessed One?" [62] Jesus said, "I am; and you will see the Son of Man seated at the right hand of the Power, and coming with the clouds of heaven."

The high priest's question names the two most important post-Easter affirmations about Jesus: Messiah and the Son of God: "Are you the Messiah, the Son of the Blessed One?" he demands. These are the titles of Jesus in the first verse of Mark's gospel.

Mark reports Jesus' ambiguous response. The Greek phrase translated as "I am" can also be translated as "Am I?" Matthew and Luke both read it as ambiguous: the former renders it as "You have said so" (Matt 26:64), and the latter as "You say that I am" (Luke 22:70). But the rest of Jesus' statement in Mark 14:62 suggests an affirmation: "*You will see the Son of Man seated at the right hand of the Power, and coming with the clouds of heaven.*" Jesus affirms that he is the Son of Man who will soon judge the authorities before whom he now stands.

The condemnation follows:

> [63] Then the high priest tore his clothes and said, "Why do we still need witnesses? [64] You have heard his blasphemy! What is your decision?" All of them condemned him as deserving death.

Did the trial happen this way? Is this the historically accurate "gist" of the event? Did the high priest and what has been called his "privy council" meet before dawn on Friday and "try" Jesus? We do not know. On historical grounds, it seems improbable that they would do so on the night of the most holy day of the Jewish year. According to the gospel of John, there was no such meeting—the condemnation of Jesus by the temple authorities occurred before he even arrived in Jerusalem (John 11:45–53).

Yet the passage in Mark accurately reflects the fact that Jesus was condemned to death by collaboration between religious and imperial authority. Not only do all the gospels say so, but so does the Jewish historian Josephus. Again, remember: temple authorities are not to be identified with the Jewish people. The crowd of

Jewish pilgrims are on the side of Jesus—that's why the authorities needed Judas.

Condemnation and Crucifixion by Roman Authority (15:1–39)

INTERROGATION BY PILATE (15:1–5)

At dawn on Friday morning, the temple authorities hand Jesus over to the Roman governor. Pilate interrogates him: "Are you the King of the Jews?" Jesus' response is ambiguous: "You say so"—that's the charge. When the chief priests continue to make other accusations, "Pilate asked him again, 'Have you no answer? See how many charges they bring against you'. But Jesus made no further reply, so that Pilate was amazed." To remain silent in the presence of authority is an act of defiance.

BARABBAS (15:6–15)

According to Mark, it was Pilate's custom each Passover to release a prisoner, "anyone for whom they asked." He offers them Jesus, but "the chief priests stirred up the crowd to have him release Barabbas" (in prison for his involvement in a violent insurrection). The crowd that asks for Barabbas is a different crowd from the one that had been on Jesus' side all week. They are gathered in a courtyard of Pilate's palace (formerly a palace of Herod the Great). Entrance was no doubt restricted.

It is a curious incident and most scholars regard it as unhistorical. It is unlikely that a Roman governor whose primary responsibility was law and order would release anybody the crowd asked for, especially an insurrectionist. We know of no such custom anywhere in the Roman Empire. But as a "parable" of what had happened by the time Mark wrote, it makes considerable sense. Pilate offered the crowd Jesus or Barabbas, one representing a non-violent challenge to Roman rule, the other offering the path of violence. By the time Mark wrote, many Jews living in the homeland had chosen the path of violence—Barabbas rather than Jesus.

The story has sometimes been read to imply that Pilate really didn't want to crucify Jesus. That is possible, but unlikely. Two first-century Jewish authors, Philo and Josephus, portray Pilate as ruthless and brutal; it seems improbable that he would be concerned with the guilt or innocence of somebody presented to him as a would-be king of the Jews. And it is possible to read the words that Mark attributes to him as taunting his Jewish subjects rather than as reluctance to commit an unjust act. In any case, Pilate orders Jesus' crucifixion.

FLOGGING, MOCK CROWNING, CRUCIFIXION (15:15–39)

Pilate has Jesus flogged. Then soldiers mockingly enthrone him. Clothing him in a purple robe (the color of royalty), they put a crown of thorns on his head and hail him as "King of the Jews." Kneeling before him, they spit on him and beat him. Their actions proclaim that *this* is what we do to kings of the Jews.

At nine in the morning, a squad of soldiers crucify Jesus, after undressing him and dividing his clothing among them by casting lots. On a placard on the cross is the charge: "The King of the Jews." On either side of him are two "bandits," a translation of a Greek word that commonly meant violent rebels—not simply "thieves" or "robbers" but resistance fighters. Recall that the Romans reserved crucifixion for those who defied their rule—they did not use it for common criminals.

Darkness comes over the whole land at noon and lasts for three hours. At three in the afternoon, Jesus dies. This is unusual: as a deterrent against rebellion, crucifixion was designed to be a lingering and tormenting death that could take a day or more. As Jesus dies, he cries out, "*Eloi, Eloi, lema sabachthani?*" Aramaic words that mean, "My God, my God, why have you forsaken me?" They are his last (and only) words from the cross in Mark.

In this part of Mark's story, we see the influence of the Old Testament at several points:

- Jesus' final words, just quoted, are from Psalm 22:1, which speaks of a righteous person undergoing extraordinary suffering and his hope for vindication.
- Psalm 22:18 is echoed in the detail of the soldiers casting lots for Jesus' garment. In the psalm, the heirs of the sufferer are so certain he is dying that they are beginning to divide up the inheritance.
- The description of "mockers" "shaking their heads" echoes Psalm 22:7.

These correlations should not be seen as predictions of what happened, as if the author of Psalm 22 was predicting details of Jesus' death. Rather, Mark is using the psalm as he tells the story.

So also the darkness at midday echoes Old Testament passages such as Exodus 10:21–23, Jeremiah 15:9, Zephaniah 1:15, Joel 2:2 and 31, Amos 8:9. They are about God's judgment—not "the last judgment" but about events within history. The darkness was not an eclipse of the sun—solar eclipses last only minutes, never three hours. Rather, Mark uses this motif to say that "this world"—the powers that killed Jesus—is being judged in his death.

> **Holy of holies:** the innermost and most sacred space in the temple; only the high priest could enter, and only on one day a year

A final symbolic detail: as Jesus dies, "the curtain of the temple was torn in two, from top to bottom." The curtain separated the most sacred part of the temple, "the holy of holies," from the rest of the temple. The "holy of holies" was understood to be the place where God's presence was most concentrated; it was so sacred that only the high priest could enter it, and on only one day each year. Whether or not the temple curtain was really torn in two, the meaning is clear. Negatively, it is a judgment against what the temple had become; positively, it proclaims that access to God is possible apart from temple. The curtain is gone.

The scene at the cross ends with a centurion exclaiming, "Truly this man was God's Son!" This is the first time in Mark's gospel that a human calls Jesus "God's Son." It happens at the crucifixion, and it is spoken by a centurion who presumably had thought of the emperor as "God's Son." Now Jesus, crucified by empire, is declared "God's Son."

Burial (15:40–47)

The rest of Mark 15 relates Jesus' burial. Joseph of Arimathea, a member of the Jewish council, asks Pilate for Jesus' body in order to give him a decent burial. The request was unusual; normally, the body of a crucified person was not released for burial; it was commonly left on the cross for some days and then, if anything was left, thrown into a common grave. As Mark tells the story, an exception was made for Jesus.

A number of women play a role in this part of the story: Mary Magdalene, Mary the mother of James the younger and of Joses, and Salome, and many others who provided for him in Galilee and followed him to Jerusalem. Mary Magdalene and Mary the mother of Joses follow Joseph to the tomb and "saw where the body was laid."

The Empty Tomb (16:1–8)

On Sunday morning, three of these women go to the tomb to anoint Jesus' body.

> [1] When the sabbath was over, Mary Magdalene, and Mary the mother of James, and Salome bought spices, so that they might go and anoint him. [2] And very early on the first day of the week, when the sun had risen, they went to the tomb. [3] They had been saying to one another, "Who will roll away the stone for us from the entrance to the tomb?" [4] When they looked up, they saw that the stone, which was very large, had already been rolled back. [5] As they entered the tomb, they saw a young man, dressed in a white robe, sitting on the right side; and they were alarmed. [6] But he said to them, "Do not be alarmed; you are looking for Jesus of Nazareth, who was crucified. He has been raised; he is not here. Look, there is the place they laid him. [7] But go, tell his disciples and Peter that he is going ahead of you to Galilee; there you will see him, just as he told you." [8] So they went out and fled from the tomb, for terror and amazement had seized them; and they said nothing to anyone, for they were afraid.

Mark's story of Easter surprises us for more than one reason:

- Its brevity—only eight verses long, compared to Matthew's twenty verses, Luke's fifty-three verses, and two chapters in John 20–21.
- Its ending, which is also the ending of his gospel: the women flee from the tomb and "said nothing to anyone, for they were afraid." This is puzzling, and it is not surprising that longer endings were added to Mark over the next century. Though printed in some Bibles, they were not originally part of Mark.

A further surprise: Mark has no appearance stories—no stories of the risen Jesus appearing to his followers, as we find in the other gospels. There is the promise of appearances: the women are told,

"Go, tell his disciples and Peter that he is going ahead of you to Galilee; *there you will see him,* just as he told you." Go back to Galilee where it all began—there you will see him. But there are no appearance stories. Why not? Did Mark not know of any? Did he know one or more appearance stories, but chose not to include them? Did he include one or more, but then the ending of his gospel got lost? All have been suggested.

But in spite of its brevity and its lack of appearance stories, Mark's Easter story is remarkably complete and filled with meaning. The women go to the tomb, expecting to find Jesus in the land of the dead—but the tomb is empty. It is empty. The resurrection is proclaimed to the women: "You are looking for Jesus of Nazareth, who was crucified. *He has been raised; he is not here.*" Note that the proclamation of his resurrection includes mention of his crucifixion. Though he was executed by the authorities, you won't find him in a tomb—he has been raised by God. Even a sealed tomb with a huge stone rolled in front of it could not contain Jesus. As Luke 24:5 puts it in his story of the empty tomb, "Why do you look for the living among the dead?"

For some Christians today, it matters greatly that the tomb really was empty and that the resurrection of Jesus involved his physical body. I have no need to argue the opposite. To become embroiled in such an argument is a distraction. Instead, I invite readers to set that question aside—to believe whatever you want about whether the tomb really was empty—and instead to ask the question of meaning: "What does the story of the empty tomb mean?"

For early Christians generally, Easter had two primary meanings. Jesus lives—he is a figure of the present, not simply of the past. And Jesus is Lord—one with God, raised to God's right hand, vindicated by God as both Lord and Christ, and thus vindicated against the powers that put him to death. All of these are present, explicitly or implicitly, in Mark's story of the empty tomb.

And so Mark's story ends. It is, as Mark says in the title to his gospel, the good news of Jesus the Messiah and the Son of God. The language proclaims the significance of Jesus for Mark and his community and for Christians ever since. In this person, we see the decisive revelation of God—of God's character and God's passion. Go back to Galilee, to the beginning of the story—there you will see him.

STUDY QUESTIONS

The purpose of this guide is to present questions on the major themes of the book in order to enhance your study of the Gospel of Mark. Marcus Borg's analysis provides a wealth of material for personal reflection and group discussion. As you read each chapter, select the areas of most interest for further exploration. At the end of each session, reflect on what new insights you have discovered and what further questions have surfaced for you.

When our own story connects with "The Story" of scripture, our lives are transformed. Thus the study questions are designed to help integrate our own experience with that of Mark's gospel. Mark's story is our story as well.

Before you begin your study of Mark, read the entire gospel. If you are participating in a study group, read Mark aloud with all the members of the group taking turns reading. Listen as if you are hearing the story for the first time. Focus on the flow of the narrative, and imagine that you are a part of the story. What are the sights, sounds, and smells that you experience?

After your reading, reflect on the following questions:
- What surprised you or was unexpected?
- What particular images, events, and characters caught your attention and stand out most vividly for you?
- What is the picture of Jesus that emerges in Mark's telling of the story?
- How would you describe the world of first century Israel?

- What preconceived notions about the gospel of Mark and the life of Jesus were either confirmed or called into question for you?
- What questions arose for you that you hope to explore further in this study?

The Collect for Proper 28 in the *Book of Common Prayer* (p. 236) provides a framework for the study of scripture. Begin each session by saying this prayer together:

> Blessed Lord, who caused all holy Scriptures to be written for our learning: Grant us so *to hear them, read, mark, learn, and inwardly digest them,* that we may embrace and ever hold fast the blessed hope of everlasting life, that you have given us in our Savior Jesus Christ; who lives and reigns with you and the Holy Spirit, one God, forever and ever. *Amen.*

Introduction

In this opening chapter, Borg identifies the distinctive features of the Gospel of Mark as the earliest written record of the life of Jesus. He presents the historical-metaphorical approach as the framework for biblical interpretation in which the historical context is considered along with multiple layers of metaphorical meaning.

In the preface, Borg states his conviction about the importance of the integration of faith and reason. He writes that "Faith without reason can become fantasy and, at its extreme, fanaticism. Reason without faith can become arid and amoral."

- How would you characterize the relationship between faith and reason—i.e., between what Borg describes as "head and heart, intellect, experience, and yearning" —in the Church and in the world today?
- What role does the integration of faith and reason play in your own faith journey?

Borg's emphasis on faith and reason comprise the basis for the two perspectives that shape the way he views scripture: the first is his Christian faith. For Borg as a Christian, "Jesus is the decisive revelation of God." Jesus shows us who God is.

- What does it mean for you to say that you are a Christian?
- What does the life of Jesus reveal to you about God?

The second perspective for Borg comes from mainstream biblical scholarship that is outside any particular religious orientation or belief. Along with Jesus, the Bible is the foundation of Christian understanding, and it is the way the Spirit of God continues to speak to us today. Furthermore, the Bible is understood as a collection of writings composed by ordinary mortals that is sacred in status and function but not in origin.

- What does it mean for your study of scripture when Borg writes that "the Bible is not to be interpreted literally, factually, and absolutely"?
- What influences have shaped your approach to scripture?
- How do you read and understand the Bible, and how has the Bible made a difference in your life?
- In what ways does God's Spirit continue to speak to us through scripture?

Within the perspective of mainstream scholarship, Mark is the "product of a developing tradition" that reflects how the significance and understanding of Jesus' life and teachings evolved after his historical life. Borg gives three examples of the development of such changes—Peter's confession, teachings about divorce and remarriage, and Jesus' entry into Jerusalem.

- How has your own understanding of Jesus evolved over time, and what has influenced your thinking?
- What are the issues that arise as we continue to adapt and apply biblical traditions about Jesus into our contemporary context?
- How do "Pre-Easter memory" and "Post-Easter interpretation" shape the gospel narrative and our understanding?

Borg also points out the importance of memory and metaphor in biblical narratives. He emphasizes that metaphorical language is not inferior to factual language but is actually more than literal because metaphor is about "the surplus of meaning." A narrative does not need to be factually true in order to contain truth.

- Some metaphors are linked with memory—i.e., with an event that actually happened such as the exodus from Egypt, the Jewish exile in Babylon, or Jesus' journey to Jerusalem. What other factual events in scripture can you name that have taken on metaphorical meaning?

- What are some events or memories from contemporary culture as well your own life that have become metaphoric?
- Other metaphorical narratives are not linked with any particular memory or actual event such as the Genesis story of Adam and Eve. Like all metaphors, their meaning has many layers but is not dependant upon the facts of what happened. Think of other examples of such metaphors in scripture and in contemporary secular culture.
- How does the use of metaphor contribute to our understanding of scripture?
- What are some metaphors that describe your own faith journey?

The historical-metaphorical approach to interpreting scripture also focuses on the context of life in the biblical era and how events have been shaped by a particular time and place. Borg outlines the historic context of the gospel of Mark in the concluding pages of the chapter.

- How does this information about the historic and cultural context of Mark contribute to your understanding of the overall narrative as well as the metaphorical implications of the text?
- How does what the events meant then, contribute to their meaning for us today?

In a similar manner, we can also look at the implications of the historical and cultural context of our own lives.

- What are the influences that have formed and informed your own life, especially your spiritual life? Consider where you live, current events, and the individuals who have had an impact on your thinking.

Chapter One: Overture and Beginning: Mark 1–3

Before you begin your discussion, read chapters 1–3 of Mark. These chapters relate the beginning of the ministry of Jesus and introduce the central themes of the gospel as a whole: the good news, following the way, and the kingdom of God.

Borg compares Mark 1:1–20 to an orchestral overture that introduces the themes or motifs of the symphony that follows. The first verse tells us immediately what the main theme is: "The beginning of the good news of Jesus Christ, the Son of God."

- How do you define the "good news"?
- Mark proclaims the *beginning* of the good news. How does this good news continue to unfold in our world and in our own lives today?
- Jesus is "Christ" and "Son of God"—the long-awaited Messiah. Borg explains that these titles had different connotations for different groups in the first-century world of Jesus and the early Christian movement. What were the expectations of the Messiah then, and what do we expect today?
- What does it mean for you that Jesus is "Christ" and "Son of God"?

The second theme, in verses 3–4, centers around the "the way" that Borg defines as a metaphor for the meaning of the gospel. He goes on to explain that the gospel as the way of Jesus is a "path and a person to be followed, and not primarily a set of beliefs to be believed."

- What is the difference between following the way of Jesus as opposed to adhering to a set of beliefs?
- How are we to conduct our daily lives in order to follow the way of Jesus?
- What are the challenges we encounter as we attempt to follow the way?
- In verse 3 we read, "prepare the way of the Lord." How are we called to prepare the way of the Lord in the world today?

Verses 4–8 introduce us to John the Baptist who is a compelling and pivotal figure in all four of the gospels. Borg calls John a "popular prophet" in the sense that he was of the people and attracted a wide following.

- What was the mission of John?
- What do you imagine it might have been like to see and hear John speak?
- What is the role of a prophet?

- Who are the prophets of our own time, especially the popular prophets, and how is their message received?
- How does John's message continue to be relevant for us today?

The baptism of Jesus by John is described in verses 9–11. (Also see Matthew 3:13–17; Luke 3:21–22; and John 1:29–34).

- Why do you think Jesus came to John to be baptized, and what do you imagine the relationship between the two men might have been?
- This is the first event in the life of Jesus that is recorded by Mark. What was the significance of his baptism for Jesus himself and for John as well?
- What is the difference between John's baptism with water and Jesus' baptism with the Holy Spirit?
- Verses 10–11 describe the dramatic vision that came to Jesus as he came up out of the water. What is the significance of the vision, particularly the fact that the vision and the words "You are my Son, the Beloved" were revealed only to Jesus?
- What does it mean for the mission of Jesus that he is God's own beloved Son and that God is well pleased with him?
- When have you had a spiritual experience, or vision, in which you felt God's presence very clearly?
- Baptism is an actual as well as a metaphorical experience. What are the metaphorical implications of Jesus' baptism as well as baptism in general?
- Recall your own baptism, and reflect on what it means for you.

Immediately after his baptism, Jesus spent forty days in the wilderness in discernment about what it meant to be God's beloved son (verses 12–13).

- The text says that the "Spirit immediately *drove*" Jesus into the wilderness. What is the significance of this strong language here?
- Why was this time imperative for Jesus, and what do you imagine were the temptations that he might have faced? (Also refer to the accounts in Matthew 4:1–11 and Luke 4:1–13.)
- The "wilderness experience" is a familiar metaphor. What does the wilderness itself represent, and what are the implications of such experiences?

- Reflect on your own wilderness experiences, and what these times have meant for you.

The first words spoken by Jesus in Mark's narrative are found in verse 15 as Jesus proclaims the central message of his ministry.

- In the text, Borg asks, "If you were to state the gospel, the heart of the Christian message, in a sentence or two, what would you say?" What is your response to this question, and how has your understanding evolved over time?

Jesus proclaims the "kingdom of God has come near."

- The kingdom of God is a metaphoric expression as well as a concrete reality. How would you define the kingdom of God, and how might our understanding today compare with that of Jesus' time?
- The kingdom of God calls for transformation of life in *this world*. What is our role in this transformation, and how have you been transformed by your life in Christ?
- Borg describes the primary features of the kingdom as peace and justice. What can we as individuals and the Church as a whole do to bring about peace and justice in our world?
- What evidence do you see of God's kingdom in the world today?

Jesus also calls us to "repent and believe."

- Borg writes that to repent is "to embark on the way of return to God by going beyond the mind that we have." What does this change of direction mean for our individual lives and our relationship with others, and how are we challenged to move outside of our normal comfort zones?
- To *believe* in the good news involves commitment to God and God's kingdom. What must we do to live out this commitment?

Mark's overture concludes with the call of the first four disciples (verses 16–20).

- What do you think compelled Simon, Andrew, James, and John to leave their families and livelihood as fishermen to follow Jesus?

- What does the metaphor of fishing for people suggest?

Verses 21–45 of Mark's first chapter describe the beginning of Jesus' public ministry as he teaches, casts out demons, and heals the sick. He also finds time for private prayer. This pattern of ministry will be repeated through the remainder of the gospel.

- As you read these verses, what is the response of the people who witness the miracles performed by Jesus?
- In verse 38, Jesus says, "Let us go on to the neighboring towns, so that I may proclaim the message there also; *for that is what I came out to do.*" What does this tell us about what Jesus understood as the focus of his ministry?
- The importance of prayer in the life of Jesus is noted in verse 35 as Jesus went alone to a secluded place to pray. How and when do you make time in our own life for prayer?

As Jesus continues his ministry in chapters 2 and 3, he soon begins to encounter opposition from various groups as his fame continues to spread throughout the countryside.

- What are the issues that are raised against Jesus, and how do these issues relate to conflict among religious groups in our own time?
- Who are the groups that opposed Jesus, and why do you think they felt threatened by his ministry?
- Why does Jesus' own family reject him (3:31–35)? What does his family and others not understand about him?

Jesus also appoints the twelve apostles "to be with him, and to be sent out to proclaim the message, and to have authority to cast out demons" (3:14–15).

- Why was it important for Jesus to have others involved in his ministry?
- How are we called to participate in Jesus' ministry today?

As you reflect on these first three chapters, what is the image of Jesus and his ministry that Mark presents for us?

Chapter Two: Parables and Miracles: Mark 4–5

Jesus continues his ministry in Galilee as he teaches and performs miracles. Read chapters 4 and 5 before you begin your study.

Jesus often taught in parables, and chapter 4 includes three parables that Jesus told to the crowds who gathered to hear him speak. Mark 4:34 states that "he did not speak to them except in parables. . . ." Borg defines parables as made-up stories that are "invitations to see something that you might not otherwise see." They are meant to be provocative and pull us in to the story for further reflection.

As you read the parables of the sower (4:3–20), the growing seed (4:26–29), and the mustard seed (4:30–32), put yourself into the stories and consider the following questions:

- What do you find in these stories that was unexpected or challenging?
- What do you think Jesus wanted his audience to know from these parables?
- The parables of the growing seed and the mustard seed are kingdom parables. What is the kingdom of God like in these stories?
- The parable of the sower is followed by an explanation (4:13–20) that was probably added later. What does this interpretation add (or detract) from your understanding of the parable?
- Parables have many layers of meaning. How do these stories continue to speak to us today?
- What are some modern-day parables that call into question accepted norms?

Verses 21–25 of chapter 4 contain a number of short sayings, or aphorisms, that were also common in Jesus' teaching. How are these teachings relevant to our lives today?

The next section of Mark consists of four mighty works of Jesus beginning with the stilling of the storm (4:35–41). This is an example of a nature miracle that Borg describes as a metaphorical narrative or parabolic narrative. The point of such stories is not whether they happened exactly as told (or if they happened at all), but *what the stories mean.*

- As you read about the stilling of the storm, imagine that you are one of the disciples in the boat as the storm begins. Describe your thoughts and feelings at the different points in the story. What is it like to be in this boat?
- How does the metaphorical meaning of "the sea" in Jesus' time enhance our understanding of the story?
- What is the metaphorical meaning of the sea for us today, and how does our contemporary understanding compare with that of the ancient worldview?
- What other metaphorical elements do you identify in this story?
- After Jesus calms the storm, he says to the disciples, "Why are you afraid? Have you still no faith?" (v. 40). What is the connection between faith and fear as seen in this event?
- What are the storms in your own life, and how has Jesus acted to calm your fears?

Chapter 5 begins with the healing of the Gerasene demoniac. In addition to being a teacher, Jesus was also well-known as an exorcist and healer. Jesus' public ministry began with the exorcism of a man with an unclean spirit (1:21–28), and Jesus' chosen apostles were given authority to cast out demons (3:15). Belief in demons and spirits that could take possession of individuals was widespread in the ancient world. As depicted in the New Testament, such spirits were opposed to God's kingdom.

- In our contemporary Western culture, we are not accustomed to thinking of individuals as being possessed by demons. As you read the account of the Gerasene demoniac, what are the metaphoric elements that you identify in this story?
- What does the Gerasene man represent for us, and how was he transformed?
- What is the significance of the fact that the unclean spirits recognize Jesus as the "Son of the Most High God" (5:7) when even Jesus' closest followers do not?
- There are many improbable and even fantastical elements in this incident that make it difficult to understand. However, paired with the previous miracle of the stilling of the storm, what do these two stories tell us about Jesus?

Read the accounts of the healing of the woman with a hemorrhage and the raising of the daughter of Jairus in 5:21–43.

- What is the effect of having these two stories intertwined in the narrative?
- How would you describe the main characters in each story, and what do they have in common? If these characters could meet, what do you imagine they would have to say to one another about Jesus?
- What do these two stories tell us about faith?
- How does the theme of faith as represented here relate to the elements of faith exemplified in the previous two stories of the stilling of the storm and the healing of the Gerasene demonic?
- After the exorcism of the Gerasene man, Jesus told him to tell his friends "how much the Lord has done for you" (5:19). Yet Jesus tells the friends of Jairus to tell no one about the healing of his daughter. How would you explain the difference?
- In both of these stories, the eyewitnesses to the events were amazed. What is our attitude about news of the seemingly miraculous events today and why?

As you reflect on the parables as well as the miracle stories in this chapter, what has been revealed to you about Jesus and his ministry that is meaningful for your own faith journey?

Chapter Three: Rejection, Miracles, and Conflict: Mark 6:1–8:21

As Jesus continues his ministry in Galilee he confronts increasing opposition from the religious establishment. Along with healings and miracles, there are also rejection, conflict, and misunderstanding. Read Mark 6:1–8:21 in preparation for your discussion.

Mark 6:1–6 relates the rejection of Jesus in his hometown of Nazareth.

- How do you imagine Jesus was formed by his experiences growing up in the small, rural village of Nazareth? How have your life and attitudes been influenced by the place where you grew up?
- Although the initial response of the inhabitants of Nazareth toward Jesus was positive, they soon "took offense at him"

(6:3), and Jesus "could do no deed of power there" (6:5). How do you account for the attitude of the people of Nazareth and the fact that Jesus' abilities were limited there?

- Jesus himself was "amazed at their unbelief" (6:6). What does this incident suggest about the connection between belief and healing?

Jesus says, "Prophets are not without honor, except in their home-town, and among their own kin, and in their own house" (6:4).

- Give further examples of how this familiar saying continues to be true. Why do we reject those who are closest to us?
- How is the theme of the rejected prophet developed in Mark's portrayal of Jesus?

In 6:7–13, Jesus sends the twelve apostles out two-by-two on a missionary journey to proclaim repentance, cast out demons, and cure the sick.

- Why do you think Jesus sent the apostles out on their own at this time?
- How do you think the apostles might have felt as Jesus sent them out and gave them authority over the unclean spirits?
- How is the sending out of the twelve a model for discipleship?

Sandwiched between the sending of the twelve and their return is the account of the death of John the Baptizer (6:14–29).

- What were the forces in play that brought about the death of John?
- How does the execution of John foreshadow the death of Jesus?

The feeding of the five thousand (6:30–44) is the second nature miracle in Mark. Mark and Matthew also record the feeding of four thousand.

- Because it is included in all four gospels, this story must have had great significance for the early Christian community. How do you think this story might have been understood at the time in comparison to how we view it today?

- Read the accounts of this story as recorded in the other gospels (Matthew 14:13–21; Luke 9:10–17; John 6:1–21) as well as the feeding of the four thousand in Mark 8:1–10 and Matthew 15:32–39. What do the similarities and differences that you notice contribute to your understanding of the event?
- What does the setting of a deserted place in Mark contribute to the implications of the story?
- When the disciples called Jesus' attention to the need to provide food for the crowd, he told them, "You give them something to eat" (6:37). What is the role of the disciples here, and what does this suggest to us about our responsibilities as followers of Jesus today?
- In the Lord's Prayer, we say, "Give us this day our daily bread." Borg notes that "real bread is central to the coming of the kingdom of God." What does this tell us about the kingdom of God, and the relationship between physical and spiritual needs?
- What does this story suggest about issues of scarcity and abundance?
- What Eucharistic themes are found in this story?
- Setting aside questions of factuality, this story has several layers of meaning and deep metaphorical implications. What is the significance of this familiar story for the Church and for you personally?

Mark 6:45–52 tells of a storm on the Sea of Galilee that is similar to a story told earlier in 4:35–41.

- Unlike the previous story, Jesus was not with the disciples when the storm arose, and they struggled to keep the boat under control in the strong winds. What does this suggest to us about the presence of Jesus in our lives?
- When Jesus got into the boat with the apostles, the wind ceased, and they were "utterly astounded, for they did not understand about the loaves, but their hearts were hardened" (6:51–52). What did they not understand, and what got in the way of their ability to comprehend?
- Matthew's account of this event adds the scene of Peter's attempt to walk across the water to Jesus (Matthew 13:28–31). What do we learn about faith here?

- What are the metaphorical elements of this event?
- Along with the loaves and fishes story, what is the picture of the apostles that emerges from this incident?

Mark 7:1–23 focuses on the debate between Jesus and the scribes and Pharisees from Jerusalem over purity issues. Here Jesus calls attention to the tension of knowing the difference between the commandment of God and human tradition.

- How does this distinction continue to be an issue in the church and in our personal lives today—i.e., how can we discern what is truly from God?
- How does Jesus expose the hypocrisy of the religious authorities in this situation?
- What is the hypocrisy that Jesus might call attention to in our faith communities today?
- In verse 15, Jesus declares that "there is nothing outside a person that by going in can defile, but the things that come out are what defile." How does this statement radically redefine purity issues, and what barriers are broken down here?
- Jesus further explains this statement to his disciples in 7:17–23. What is the relationship between external practice and our internal state?
- Purity issues are not a part of contemporary culture in the same way as in the ancient world, but what are the metaphorical implications for us now?

Jesus now moves outside Galilee into Gentile territory where he performs an exorcism for the daughter of a Gentile woman (7:24–30).

- At first Jesus refused to help the woman's daughter. What caused Jesus to change his mind?
- What are the issues today that challenge us to change our thinking, and what gets in the way of our resolve to bring about change?
- How would you describe the Syrophoenician woman, and what do we learn about faith from her?
- Reflect on this story in light of the previous controversies over purity laws. What further barriers does Jesus break down here,

and what are the barriers that we are called to confront in our world today?

This section ends as it began with those closest to Jesus not understanding him or his ministry. In 8:11–21, the Pharisees demand a sign in order to test Jesus, and Jesus questions why his disciples still do not understand.

- Jesus has performed many healing miracles as well as other deeds of power. What more do the religious establishment as well as the followers of Jesus expect from him? What are the signs we continue to ask for today?
- How do you explain the fact that the apostles, who were with Jesus daily, did not understand what was happening before their very eyes? What gets in the way of our understanding today?

As you reflect on the events presented in this chapter, what do we learn about Jesus himself and his ministry?

- What are the themes that Mark continues to develop?
- What is the picture that emerges of the apostles, and how would you describe their relationship with Jesus?

Chapter Four: From Galilee to Jerusalem: Mark 8:22–10:52

This is a pivotal section in Mark's gospel as Jesus is revealed as the Messiah and begins his journey to Jerusalem. He speaks about his coming betrayal, death, and resurrection, and continues teaching his disciples about what it means to be a follower on "the way." Pay particular attention to the development of these themes as you read Mark 8:22–10:52.

The three Passion predictions in Mark's gospel follow a pattern of the prediction itself, followed by the misunderstanding of the apostles and a discourse on true discipleship.

The first prediction follows Peter's confession in 8:27–30 that Jesus is the Messiah.

Although the opening verse of Mark's gospel proclaims Jesus as the Son of God, Peter's declaration marks the first time a follower of Jesus affirms that Jesus is the Messiah. Jesus himself does not make this claim in Mark. What implications does this have for our understanding of Jesus and his ministry?

- What do you think Peter and the other disciples expected the Messiah to be, and in comparison, how do we understand the role of the Messiah today?
- After this revelation, Jesus "*sternly* ordered them not to tell anyone about him." On several occasions of healing miracles, Jesus also warned those involved not to tell anyone. What was the purpose and effect of this "messianic secret"?
- What is your response to Jesus' question of "Who do *you* say that I am?"

Peter's confession is followed by Jesus' first declaration of his coming Passion (8:31), whereupon Peter pulls him aside and rebukes him (8:32).

- Why do you think Peter reacted so strongly to Jesus' words?
- How do we respond today to the fact that Jesus had to die such a horrible death?
- In turn, Jesus rebukes Peter in front of the other disciples saying that Peter is focused on human rather than divine things (8:33). What can explain Jesus' strong response to Peter—even calling him Satan?
- What were the divine things that Jesus wanted Peter to see, and what got in the way of Peter's understanding?
- How can we discern in our own lives what is from God and what is not?
- How do you imagine Peter might have felt throughout this scene?

Following this exchange is the first discourse on discipleship (8:34–38).

- Jesus declares that those who would follow him must "deny themselves and take up their cross and follow me" (8:34). Taking up the cross has become a familiar metaphor. What are some of the words and images that are associated with "the cross"?
- How is the meaning of the phrase "take up your cross" different for us today than in the context of Jesus' world? What are your own crosses?

- What does Jesus mean by the paradoxical saying that one must lose one's life in order to save it (8:35–37), and what does this have to do with our lives today?

The second Passion prediction and misunderstanding is found in 9:31–32. Here we read that the disciples "did not understand what he was saying and were afraid to ask him."

- Why do you think they were afraid to ask Jesus, and how do our own fears keep us from seeking the truth?

The teaching that follows this prediction (9:33–37) comes as the disciples argue over which one of them was the greatest. Jesus once again presents a paradox: "Whoever wants to be first must be last of all and servant of all" (9:35).

- What words and images do you associate with servanthood, and how might our contemporary understanding be different than that of Jesus' time?
- How do servant and servanthood serve as metaphors?
- How is Jesus a model of servanthood, and how are we to follow this example in our own lives?
- Who has been a servant to you, and when have you been a servant to others?
- Jesus also put a little child among them saying that whoever welcomes a child in his name also welcomes "the one who sent me." What does this further suggest about discipleship, and why do you think Jesus used a child as an example?

The final Passion prediction in 10:32–34 is the longest and most detailed.

- Why do you think Jesus continued to tell the disciples what was ahead, and why did they continue to ignore his words?
- Put yourself in Jesus' place and imagine what it might have been like for him to predict his own death and rising again.

The third teaching about discipleship comes as James and John come forward asking to sit beside Jesus when he comes into his glory (10:37). As you read Jesus' reply in 10:38–45 consider the following questions:

- How are baptism and the cup used here as metaphors for following the way of Jesus?

- What does Jesus tell us about true greatness here?
- Who are some individuals who exemplify for you the qualities of greatness that Jesus describes?
- What do James and John still not understand?

As you reflect on all three of the discipleship discourses, how would you summarize what it means to follow Jesus on "the way"?

- What are the challenges of following Jesus?
- What changes are we called to make in our lives in order to follow these teachings of Jesus?
- What is revealed about the disciples in these passages, and in what ways do you identify with them?

This section of Mark also includes the Transfiguration (9:2–10)—a mysterious and mystical event that took place between the first and second Passion predictions. (This event is also found in Matthew 17:1–8 and Luke 9:28–36.)

- How is this event connected to the baptism of Jesus as well as with Jesus' Passion predictions?
- What is the significance of the appearance of Elijah and Moses with Jesus? (Refer to Luke 9:31.)
- Our desire to erect memorials to commemorate important events is reflected in Peter's suggestion to build three dwellings on the mountain. As you think about contemporary memorials, what do they say about what we value?
- The voice from the cloud said, "This is my Son, the Beloved. Listen to him!" (v. 7). What were Peter, James, and John to listen to, and what are we to listen for today as well?
- Afterward, Jesus reinforced the Messianic secret as "he ordered them to tell no one about what they had seen, *until after the Son of Man had risen from the dead*" (9:9). What does this tell us about the significance of this event at the time, and what does the Transfiguration mean for us today?

After Jesus and the apostles came down from the mountain, we read that the apostles did not understand what Jesus meant about rising from the dead (9:10). Their inability to understand is certainly reasonable since no one had ever risen from the dead before.

- What questions do we continue to have today about the meaning of the death and resurrection of Jesus?
- Borg makes the case that Jesus' death is a means of liberation for others and is not a substitutionary sacrifice for sin. How are we liberated by the death of Jesus?

Chapter 10 of Mark includes teachings about wealth in the story of the rich man (10:17–22) and Jesus' further commentary on the right use of riches in 10:23–31.

- According to this story, what is essential in order to follow Jesus, particularly with regard to material wealth?
- What do you make of the fact that the text tells us that Jesus loved the man in 10:21?
- How do we view wealth and the wealthy in our own culture, and how do our attitudes contrast with those of Jesus' time?
- How are we called to use our financial and material resources to reflect the values of God's kingdom?

This section of Mark began with the healing of an unnamed blind man at Bethsaida (8:22–26) and ends with the restoration of sight to Bartimaeus (10:46–52).

- What do you notice as you compare the two accounts?
- On a metaphorical level, what do these stories suggest about our own blind spots with regard to our understanding of Jesus and his call to us—how do our eyes need to be opened?
- After he was healed, Bartimaeus immediately followed Jesus on the way. In light of Jesus' teachings on discipleship and his Passion predictions, what did it mean for Bartimaeus to follow on "the way"?

In this section of Mark, Jesus begins his journey to Jerusalem where he will face suffering and death and will rise again.

- What is the significance of Jerusalem on both a literal and metaphorical level for Jesus then and for us today?
- What else have you learned about Jesus from these readings?

Chapter Five: Jerusalem, Execution, and Resurrection: Mark 11–16

The last six chapters of Mark's gospel record the events of Jesus' final week as he entered Jerusalem where he faced opposition, betrayal, and finally death and resurrection.

Chapters 11–13 tell of Jesus' ministry in Jerusalem while chapters 14–16 relate his arrest, trial, crucifixion, and the discovery of the empty tomb.

- As you read chapters 11–16, put yourself into the events as they unfold in this drama and pay close attention to the specific words and actions of Jesus himself. What do we learn about Jesus and how he understood his ministry in these final days?
- What are the metaphorical meanings that are related with the events?
- Reflect on how we observe these events through our worship. How does our liturgy contribute to our understanding of the events?
- This is the most sacred week of the Christian year. What symbols, etc., are most meaningful for you?

Jesus' final week began with his triumphal entry into Jerusalem (11:1–11). Imagine that you are among the crowd that cried "Hosanna!" as Jesus passed by.

- Borg describes this event as a pre-planned public demonstration. In light of the political context of the Roman occupation of Israel, what do you think the people who welcomed Jesus expected of him at this time?
- As a symbolic act, what did Jesus intend, particularly in light of his teachings about the kingdom of God?
- How do we understand this event today?

The next day Jesus returned to Jerusalem and went to the temple where he cast out the moneychangers (11:15–19).

- This so-called cleansing of the temple was also a premeditated, deliberate act on the part of Jesus. What were the issues that Jesus was protesting, and how are they still relevant today?

- Throughout his ministry Jesus called attention to injustice and hypocrisy. What are the areas of injustice that we are called to act against today?
- Considered together, what were the intentions and effects of the entry into Jerusalem and the cleansing of the temple?
- The cleansing of the temple is sandwiched between the incident of the cursing of the fig tree (11:12–14; 11:20–24) which further emphasizes the intent of Jesus' actions in the temple. Borg explains that on a metaphorical level the tree symbolizes the barrenness of the temple and all that it represents. What are fruits that we are called to produce as individuals and in our faith communities today?

Mark 11:27–13:2 presents a series of conflicts in which Jesus is questioned by members of the religious establishment as they attempt to discredit him. As you read this section notice how Jesus skillfully turns questions around so that his detractors incriminate themselves while the crowd looks on with amazement and delight. What is revealed in these confrontations about Jesus, his ministry and the forces that conspired against him?

- How is the authority of the religious establishment called into question in 11:27–33?
- The Parable of the Wicked Tenants (12:1–12) describes a business arrangement that was common in Jesus' time as the owner of a vineyard leased his property to tenants who would not pay the required rents. How is the murder of the vineyard owner's son turned against the religious authorities?
- The Herodians and Pharisees ask Jesus whether it is lawful to pay taxes to Caesar (12:13–17). What did the Herodians and Pharisees hope to accomplish with this question, and how did Jesus entrap them?
- The Sadducees present Jesus with a convoluted situation about the afterlife (12:18–27). How does Jesus expose the ridiculousness of the Sadducees' question, and what does he reveal about God and life after death here?
- In contrast to those who were trying to entrap Jesus, the scribe in 12:28–34 was impressed with Jesus and asked what was the

greatest commandment. When the scribe affirmed Jesus' response about loving God and loving neighbor, Jesus replied, "You are not far from the kingdom of God." What does this reveal about the kingdom of God?

- How does the riddle about the Messiah and the Son of David further delight the crowd?
- In 12:38–40, Jesus strongly criticizes the scribes who put on pious airs in public yet take advantage of the poor. How is the hypocrisy of the scribes further indicted by the actions of the poor widow in 12:41–44?
- As you reflect on these confrontations, what are the issues that are raised, and how do they continue to be present in the world today?

Following Jesus' warning of the destruction of the temple (13:1–2), the sayings in 13:3–37 are known as the "little apocalypse" in which Jesus reveals signs that the end times are near.

- As you read Jesus' words, what is the world like here, and how are the events described a reflection of the political situation of Jesus' own time?
- What is the relevance of these words for us today, especially the parable about the need to be watchful in 13:32–37?

On Jesus' fourth day in Jerusalem, the plot to betray him is put into action as Judas conspires with the chief priests (14:1–2, 10–11), and an unnamed woman anoints Jesus.

- What do you think motivated Judas to betray Jesus?
- When the woman anointed Jesus with costly ointment, Jesus praised her actions saying, "wherever the good news is proclaimed in the whole world, what she has done will be told in remembrance of her" (14:9). What did this woman understand about the ministry of Jesus that Judas and the other disciples did not? What are the qualities of discipleship taught by Jesus that the woman exemplifies, and how is she a model for us today?

In 14:12–25, Jesus celebrates the Passover meal with his disciples. At this time, Jesus institutes what we have come to know as the Eucharist (14:22–25).

- What is the nature of the covenant that is sealed with this meal?
- What did this meal signify for Jesus himself?
- What is the significance of this sacrament for you personally?
- What are some of the metaphorical meanings of the last supper?

After the meal, Jesus and the disciples go to the Mount of Olives where Jesus foretells the denial of Peter and the other apostles (14:26–31). He prays at Gethsemane as the disciples with him fall asleep (14:32–42).

- How would you characterize Jesus' prayers at this time?
- What is the "cup" that Jesus asks God to remove? (Also refer back to 10:38–39.)
- What is the significance of the fact that the disciples are unable to remain awake with him?

As you read the betrayal and arrest of Jesus (14:43–52) as well as his trial before the high priest (14:53–65) and appearance before Pilate (15:1–20), contrast Jesus' behavior and demeanor with that of his accusers.

- What were the forces that collaborated to bring about the trial and execution of Jesus, and how are these same influences still at work in the world today?
- How does Jesus respond to his accusers, and how would you describe his actions throughout his ordeal?
- What is revealed about Jesus through these events? How does he assert his authority?
- What is the significance of the release of Barabbas in the context of the political climate of the time?
- How would you describe Pilate and his role in the proceedings, and why was Pilate "amazed" by Jesus?

In 14:66–72, we read the account of Peter's betrayal as foretold by Jesus. Put yourself in Peter's place and imagine how he must have felt.

- How do you think his denial of Jesus shaped the rest of his life and ministry?
- How do we deny Jesus in our own lives today?

The crucifixion and burial of Jesus are told in 15:21–47.

- As you notice the details of these events, such as the darkness at mid-day, identify some of the metaphoric elements and the meaning those details have for us now.
- The only words that Jesus says on the cross in Mark's gospel echo Psalm 22: "My God, my God, why have you forsaken me?" (15:34). What is the effect of these words as we read them today?
- As Jesus dies, the Roman centurion who was present declares, "Truly this man was God's son" (15:39). What do you think prompted a Gentile soldier to make this proclamation? What is the irony here?

Mark's resurrection story is the shortest of all the Gospel accounts (16:1–8). Once again the women who were present at the scene of the crucifixion play the major role.

- What is surprising and unexpected in Mark's account?
- What is the effect of the final verse in which the women flee from the tomb seized with "terror and amazement"? How does this story continue to inspire fear and amazement?
- What is the meaning of the empty tomb for you?
- If the metaphorical aspects of Jesus' death and resurrection are considered, how do we participate in Jesus dying and rising again—i.e., what needs to die and be reborn into a new way in your own life? How is Jesus' teaching that we must lose our lives in order to save them reflected here?
- How has the world been changed by what happened on that long ago Sunday morning?

As you reflect on the events of Jesus' crucifixion and resurrection, what stands out most vividly for you? What new insights do you have?

In Conclusion

Now that you have completed your study of the gospel of Mark, reflect on the following questions.

- In the first chapter of the book, Borg notes the distinctive characteristics of Mark. What was most distinctive or memorable about this gospel for you?

- What new insights do you have about Jesus and his ministry—who is Jesus for you now?
- A major portion of Mark is devoted to the discourses on discipleship. What have you learned about following on "the way," and how have you been called to follow Jesus?
- In addition to following on "the way," Borg developed the themes of the good news and the kingdom of God. What new insights do you have about these themes as well?
- Borg also emphasized the importance of metaphorical meaning in scripture. What metaphor(s) describe your own experience of this study of Mark?
- Mark's story is ultimately our story as well. How have you felt your own experience connecting with that of the Gospel, and what difference has this made on your faith journey?

NOTES

1. David F. Ford, "The Bible, the World, and the Church I," in *The Report of the Lambeth Conference 1998* (ed. J. Mark Dyer et al.; Harrisburg, Pa.: Morehouse Publishing, 1999), 332.
2. "The Anglican Church has always existed in a context of rival ways of ordering the Church. On the one hand it has refused an authoritarian solution, where one central authority holds out the attractive possibility of getting rid of the messiness of debate, dissent, and rival interpretations of scripture by pronouncements and commands that permit no argument. On the other hand, it has resisted the sort of diversity in which everyone is free to do according to their own interpretation and conscience, and no one is ultimately accountable to anyone else" (Ford, 367).
3. *The Gospel of Mark* (Sonoma, Calif.: Polebridge Press, 1990), 3.
4. Verna J. Dozier, *The Dream of God: A Call to Return* (New York: Seabury Classics, 2006).
5. Marcus J. Borg and John Dominic Crossan, *The Last Week: What the Gospels Really Teach About Jesus's Final Days in Jerusalem* (New York: Harper Collins, 2006).

FURTHER READING

An excellent study Bible with introductory essays and copious footnotes on each page is *The New Interpreter's Study Bible* (NRSV).

Gospel Parallels: A Comparison of the Synoptic Gospels, ed. by B. H. Throckmorton (Thomas Nelson Publishers: Nashville).

The New Interpreter's Bible, vol. 8 (on Matthew and Mark; Abingdon Press: Nashville).

Eugene Boring, *Mark: A Commentary* (New Testament Library; Westminster John Knox: Louisville).

Adela Yarbro Collins, *The Beginning of the Gospel* (Wipf and Stock).

John R. Donahue and Daniel J. Harrington, *The Gospel of Mark* (Sacra Pagina, The Liturgical Press).

Daryl D. Schmidt, *The Gospel of Mark* (Polebridge Press: Santa Rosa, CA).

Excellent one-volume commentaries on the Bible as a whole include:
New Jerome Biblical Commentary, 3rd edition
Harper Collins Bible Commentary, rev. ed.

ABOUT THE AUTHOR

Marcus Borg is Canon Theologian at Trinity Episcopal Cathedral in Portland, OR. Internationally known in both academic and church circles as a biblical and Jesus scholar, he was Hundere Chair of Religion and Culture in the Philosophy Department at Oregon State University until his retirement in 2007.

He is the author of eighteen books, including *Jesus: A New Vision* (1987) and the best-seller *Meeting Jesus Again for the First Time* (1994); *The God We Never Knew* (1997); *The Meaning of Jesus: Two Visions* (1999); *Reading the Bible Again for the First Time* (2001), and *The Heart of Christianity* (2003), both best-sellers. His newest books are *Jesus: Uncovering the Life, Teachings and Relevance of a Religious Revolutionary* (2006), a *New York Times* Best-Seller; *Conversations with Scripture: Mark* (2009); and three books co-authored with John Dominic Crossan, *The Last Week* (2006), *The First Christmas* (2007), and *The First Paul* (2009).

His next book will be a novel, *Time After Time*, to be published in early winter '10.

Described by *The New York Times* as "a leading figure in his generation of Jesus scholars," he has appeared on NBC's "Today Show" and "Dateline," PBS's "Newshour," ABC's "Evening News" and "Prime Time" with Peter Jennings, NPR's "Fresh Air" with Terry Gross, and several National Geographic programs.

A Fellow of the Jesus Seminar, he has been national chair of the Historical Jesus Section of the Society of Biblical Literature and co-chair of its International New Testament Program Committee, and is past president of the Anglican Association of Biblical Scholars. His work has been translated into eleven languages: German, Dutch, Korean, Japanese, Chinese, Indonesian, Italian, Spanish, Portugese, Russian, and French. His doctor's degree is from Oxford University, and he has lectured widely overseas (England, Scotland, Austria, Germany, Belgium, Hungary, Israel, and South Africa) and in North America, including the Chautauqua and Smithsonian Institutions.

ALSO IN THE ANGLICAN ASSOCIATION OF BIBLICAL SCHOLARS STUDY SERIES

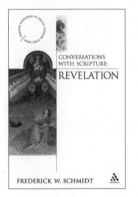

Conversations with Scripture: REVELATION

"If ever theological scholarship met the laity with grace and respect, it is here in this volume. . . . I was charmed; I was instructed; I was deeply, deeply comforted by this book. Buy it, read it, and then take it to your heart for understanding."
—Phyllis Tickle, compiler, *The Divine Hours*

"This is an important start to a most welcome series. Schmidt is a gracious and experienced teacher. He knows what false expectations his readers are likely to bring to the reading of Revelation, and offers just what we need for an encounter with the book that is honest to the text and to ourselves. . . . Schmidt's book will be widely used; and deserves to be."
—Robin Griffin-Jones, author of *The Gospel According to Paul: The Creative Genius Who Brought Jesus to the World*

 Morehouse Publishing

Morehouse books are available from Episcopal and online booksellers, or directly from the publisher at 800-242-1918 or online at www.churchpublishing.org.

ALSO IN THE ANGLICAN ASSOCIATION OF BIBLICAL SCHOLARS STUDY SERIES

Conversations with Scripture: THE LAW

"Kevin Wilson's introductory exposition of biblical Law is a must read. Unusually wide-ranging and broadly informative for a book of its size, it is jam-packed with information about the Torah's commandments, sacrifices, rituals, and theology. Wilson works hard to explain clearly how we hear God's Word today in these texts of the Law."
—Stephen L. Cook, Department of Old Testament, Virginia Theological Seminary

"Fresh insights into the meaning of the Law—and how Exodus and Leviticus provide guidelines for ethical behavior that helped shape a covenant community."
—*Diocesan Dialogue*, September 2006

"This addition to the series breaks new ground. This is a gem for adult education."
—*The Living Church*, November 2006

ⲘＰ | Morehouse Publishing

Morehouse books are available from Episcopal and online booksellers, or directly from the publisher at 800-242-1918 or online at www.churchpublishing.org.

ALSO IN THE ANGLICAN ASSOCIATION OF BIBLICAL SCHOLARS STUDY SERIES

Conversations with Scripture:
THE PARABLES

The parables are vivid, rich, arresting stories that make us think, and teach us lessons about our relationship with God and others. From talents to mustard seeds, from shepherds to Samaritans, William Brosend shows how Jesus used common reference points to teach important truths.

MP | Morehouse Publishing

Morehouse books are available from Episcopal and online booksellers, or directly from the publisher at 800-242-1918 or online at www.churchpublishing.org.